I0800839

IMAGES
of America

MILWAUKEE POLICE DEPARTMENT

OFFICER AND CHILD. A traffic officer holds on tightly to little Kathleen Zur, daughter of Otto H. Zur. They appear in several photographs taken on January 20, 1945, for a departmental series featuring local children to deliver messages promoting their safety and welfare.

On the cover: Motorcycle men from the Milwaukee Police Department's Traffic Bureau were photographed in the summer of 1933 on a winding, densely treed stretch in Milwaukee's Lake Park that was later named East Ravine Road. (Courtesy of the Milwaukee Police Historical Society.)

IMAGES
of America

MILWAUKEE POLICE DEPARTMENT

Maralyn A. Wellauer-Lenius

ARCADIA
PUBLISHING

ISBN 978-0-7385-5172-2

Published by Arcadia Publishing
Charleston, South Carolina

Printed in the United States of America

Library of Congress Catalog Card Number: 2007933286

For all general information contact Arcadia Publishing at:
Telephone 843-853-2070
Fax 843-853-0044
E-mail sales@arcadiapublishing.com
For customer service and orders:
Toll-Free 1-888-313-2665

Visit us on the Internet at www.arcadiapublishing.com

I dedicate this work to my father, George R. Wellauer, whose enduring love and gentle persuasion always encouraged me to reach higher. He left me with a lasting admiration and deep appreciation for his unceasing sense of duty, honor, and tradition. Also to my mother, Maude W. (Nelson) Wellauer, a sharp lady and devoted policeman's wife, who frequently let me know, while I was growing up, how special it was to be a policeman's daughter. Both led by example and with generosity, instilled in me the virtues of honesty and integrity, for which I am always grateful. I owe them everything.

Contents

Acknowledgments		6
Foreword		7
Introduction		9
1.	Before 1901	13
2.	From 1901 to 1919	31
3.	The 1920s	45
4.	The 1930s	55
5.	The 1940s	77
6.	The 1950s	87
7.	The 1960s	99
8.	The 1970s	111
9.	From 1980 to the Present	117
Afterword		126
Bibliography		127

ACKNOWLEDGMENTS

My grateful thanks are extended to Lt. Stephen R. Basting, recruit coordinator and instructor at the Milwaukee Police Safety Academy and vice president of the Milwaukee Police Historical Society. He frequently took time out of his very busy schedule to accommodate my requests. His enthusiasm from the start let me know this book could be written.

I owe a deep debt of gratitude to all members, past and present, of the Milwaukee Police Historical Society, keepers of the flame, without whose generosity of spirit this project would not have been possible. All photographs used in this book were carefully selected from their vast collection, unless otherwise credited. Thanks also to those who shared invaluable firsthand memories of days on the job and for general assistance, in particular Sgt. Frank J. Drezek (retired), Sgt. Robert L. Gersonde (retired), Deputy Inspector Craig V. Hasting (retired), and officer Kathy R. Schult.

Many thanks go to Sgt. Kenneth S. Henning, Milwaukee Police Department Public Information Office, for his online biographies of the chiefs, and to Diane Lardinois, Milwaukee Police Department graphics designer, for patiently scanning. For additional photographs, suggestions, and expertise, thanks to Deputy Chief William E. Gielow (retired); for scans and prints, Rose Fortier, photo librarian, Humanities Department, Milwaukee Public Library; Sarah Johnson, photo archivist, *Milwaukee Journal Sentinel*; Steven Daily, curator of research collections, Milwaukee County Historical Society; Lisa Marine, business manager, Wisconsin Historical Society; Joann Powell, vice president, Zimmerman Architectural Studios, Inc.; Marjorie Strong, assistant librarian, Vermont Historical Society; and Orson Kingsley, research center librarian, Henry Sheldon Museum.

Thanks also go to William J. Jackson, archives manager, Harley-Davidson Motor Company, for identifications; to Ron and Carline Zabler, of Color Prints, Inc., Milwaukee, for expertly adding new life to old images and turning negatives into positives; and to Mary A. Canter and Anne Morton for their suggestions and advice.

And last, but never least, to my husband, Brian J. Lenius, kudos for his careful editing and all the "above and beyond the call of duty" tasks performed at the midnight hour. He is the most faithful supporter of all my work.

Because I feel strongly about the need to preserve and conserve the department's history, 50 percent of the proceeds from the sale of this book will be donated to the Milwaukee Police Historical Society to help fund and support future projects.

FOREWORD

During the early 1990s, after many years of rescuing valuables from the trash and squirreling away artifacts, several members assigned to the Milwaukee Police Safety Academy aspired to create a historical display to be housed at the training academy on Teutonia Avenue. Academy directors, specifically Inspectors Leonard W. Ziolkowski and Joseph A. Kalivoda, provided leadership and administrative support. The society is grateful to them. The historical display soon evolved into a greater venture, an incorporated historical society (1996) complete with supporting legislation from the Milwaukee Common Council (2004).

The Milwaukee Police Historical Society was established to promote and preserve the rich history of the Milwaukee Police Department and to educate the public in matters regarding law enforcement ideals and its heritage. It encourages an appreciation of history among all members of the Milwaukee Police Department, past, present, and future. The society strives to increase awareness of police history in Milwaukee through displays, publications such as this book, tours, lectures, and meetings. The goal is to foster communication among other historical organizations in and around Milwaukee County.

In addition to expressing our appreciation to the current members of the society's board of directors, we would also like to thank past members Inspector Dean Collins, Sgt. Marvin S. Labecki, Lt. Ronald J. Rebernick, Deputy Inspector Raymond Sucik, and Deputy Inspector James Warren.

The Milwaukee Police Historical Society is pleased to share its resources with the author, Maralyn A. Wellauer-Lenius, and Arcadia Publishing to produce *Milwaukee Police Department*. It is our sincere desire that, after viewing these photographs, readers will recognize the dedication of the men and women of the Milwaukee Police Department and how grateful we are for their commitment and sacrifice.

—The Milwaukee Police Historical Society

TRAINING SCHOOL. The Milwaukee Police Department established the nation's first formal officer training school in May 1923 "for the purpose of education and instruction of all members of the department in matters pertaining and essential to services." Lessons were frequently laced with strong moral overtones, as demonstrated in this 1926 photograph, "Your Character is your Capital. Deal honorably with all persons and hold your word sacred. Obedience to Law is Liberty."

"COSSACKS?" In January 1929, four mounted policemen were assigned to direct traffic in downtown Milwaukee. Mayor Daniel W. Hoan was against the deployment, which cost around $5,000. He called the mounted police "Cossacks." Fellow detractors also objected, adding that horses were "dumb beasts, clumsy in traffic, and a great expense." However, supporters believed that horses would be an aid to traffic control, and they eventually prevailed. This photograph was taken on the Memorial Bridge.

INTRODUCTION

The remarkable story of the Milwaukee Police Department (MPD) is replete with larger-than-life chiefs, landmark achievements, and nationwide firsts. A formidable institution today, the department serves and protects 574,000 citizens, maintains seven district stations, and employs 2,000. This dynamic department rose from humble beginnings.

When Milwaukee was just a village, a lone marshal, assisted by a small band of constables and night watchmen, enforced the law. Nine years after becoming a city in 1846, Milwaukee was a wild and lawless place. A rash of thefts, murders, and arsons fueled an outcry that forced city officials to consider a permanent police force. Mayor James B. Cross responded by abolishing the office of city marshal and appointing William Beck as chief of police. One month later, on October 4, 1855, the Milwaukee Common Council passed an ordinance creating the MPD. The *Milwaukee Daily Sentinel* reported that the council confirmed "the nominations made by the Mayor and Chief of Police of seven of the ten Policemen authorized by the new ordinance," two per city ward. The three vacancies left were filled soon thereafter. The men were chosen on the basis of their size and fighting ability. The chief's annual salary was fixed at $800, and patrolmen were paid $460. There was roughly one policeman for every 3,000 citizens.

The first patrolmen had no uniforms, stars, or vehicles. They were identified only by the gold-lettered armbands they wore that read, "Milwaukee Police." Later star badges were worn, but patrolmen displayed them only when necessary to confirm their authority.

Beck located the first station (or watch) house in the basement of a building (formerly Alcott's Pharmacy) on Wisconsin Street, between Main and East Water Streets. In August 1857, his men moved into a two-story brick building on Broadway Street, just off Mason Street. It housed the Central Police Station, sheriff's office, and county jail. There was a spacious hall on the first floor with seven cells and six large cells in the basement. Beck's office was near the entrance, and there was also a bedroom for the station keeper. The police court was on the second floor.

By 1859, the mayor was allowed by state law to appoint the police chief. This politicized the position and created a situation that invited turmoil every few years. Whenever a new mayor was elected, it was common for the chief and several of his men to resign. At the first opportunity, the mayor then appointed "his" men.

After Beck's appointment, the city enjoyed a period of relative peace and quiet. Five years later, police salaries doubled and additional personnel were recruited. Beck resigned after his first term following a disagreement with Mayor James S. Brown over riot control.

Col. Walter Sheldon Johnson, a railroad man from Vermont, became chief in October 1861. During his brief term, the city developed a reputation as an easy place for gamblers and other undesirables to ply their trades. He left office and moved to St. Paul, Minnesota.

Brown appointed Herman L. Page the third chief of police in 1862. He was considered to be a man of exemplary integrity and ethics with great will and nerve. Page was said to be "one of the most efficient officials the country ever possessed." His old friend, Beck, was first lieutenant, and Peter Smith was second lieutenant.

After Page, Beck returned to serve his second term from 1863 to 1878. The force was growing—from 42 to 67 in 1874. Reportedly, the patrolmen-to-citizen ratio in Milwaukee was three times greater than in New York City.

Mayor John Black next appointed Chief Daniel Kennedy. The political spoils system, still in effect, resulted in Kennedy dismissing 25 patrolmen, whose only disqualification was that they were Republicans. Kennedy's annual salary was $2,000 per year, compared with the county sheriff's salary of $5,000. The force increased to 127 by the end of Kennedy's term.

Chief Robert Wason (also Wasson) was appointed in March 1882. During his short term that ended in 1884, Wason was credited with ending a profitable, illegal lottery operating in the city. Mayor Emil Wallber then appointed Lemuel Ellsworth chief in 1884. Wallber subsequently accused him of "lack of courtesy and neglect of duty" and questioned the efficiency of the department. Ellsworth resigned in 1885 and was succeeded by Florian J. Ries.

A new Central Police Station on Oneida Street (now East Wells Street) and North Broadway Street, a real jewel in the crown of the department, was opened on March 10, 1885. Ninety-four men and two boys were employed as officers, station keepers, detectives, patrolmen, and telegraphers. The police department had three horse-drawn vehicles, one for each precinct station. In May 1886, riots (known as the Great Labor Strike) broke out in Milwaukee. Frenzied mobs of anarchists, demanding an eight-hour workday, became particularly abusive to police, declaring them "enemies of the people." The military had to be called in to restore order.

The department began the practice of photographing prisoners during Ries's term. Previously, identification was dependent on officers' memories. The Fire and Police Commission was created in 1885. Thereafter, only the commissioners could hire or fire the chief. They fired Ries, the last chief appointed under the old spoils system, in 1888.

German-born John T. Janssen took over the chief's office at age 33 in 1888 and served for a lengthy 33 years. He is credited for bringing stability, leadership, and discipline to the department. When he assumed the position, there were only three stations, 2 lieutenants, 10 detectives, and 150 patrolmen. When he retired, there were five stations and 694 men on the force, including 588 patrolmen. Janssen was the first chief to take a firm stand against political interference. Once, when the mayor demanded his resignation, Janssen fired a letter back simply stating, "Go to hell."

In 1892, the MPD was called one of the finest forces in the country. Patrolmen by now were expected "to know something about every subject in the gamut of knowledge." They had to work longer hours than anywhere else in the country. Day men were on duty for 11 hours, with one hour off for dinner and supper. Patrolmen were often detailed for special duties at theaters, weddings, and balls, adding three to six hours to their already long workdays. They were expected to protect a population of 220,000 and cover an area of over 23 square miles.

Civil service reforms in 1894 helped the fire and police department. For the first time, candidates between the ages of 25 and 35 were tested for physical strength, capacity, activity, and educational qualities. Men had to be over five feet nine inches tall, weigh more than 155 pounds, and have no criminal convictions.

Milwaukee had an unusually low crime rate for a city of its size. Only one "cold-blooded" murder was reported in 1894, with seven more cases of homicide resulting from drunken brawls. Milwaukee police occasionally captured desperate criminals who were just passing through town. Detective Frank Miller captured Patrick Crowe, a train robber and jewel thief, when he attended the Wisconsin State Fair. The same year, police arrested Richard Lennox, a notorious check forger and swindler. More often, criminals were arrested for petty offenses, such as horse stealing, shooting within city limits, incorrigibility, and leaving horses unhitched. An increase in bicycle violation ordinances was reported at the end of the decade. Of the 5,868 prisoners arrested in

1897, 644 were women. Still, police work was grueling and exhausting. When 15 patrolmen tendered their resignations in 1899, they cited overwork as the reason.

At the beginning of the 20th century, many changes were introduced to modernize the department, improve efficiency, and provide discipline. These included the first police band in America (1898), the first police surgeon (1902), fingerprinting (1907), and the Policemen's Protective Association (1909). In 1910, the MPD first used motorized ambulances, organized the first motorcycle patrol, and closed down the thriving red-light district on River Street (later Edison Street) near city hall. Traffic "post men" were assigned to posts on busy street corners. A newly designed badge replaced the star, a new uniform was introduced, and there were several improvements in communications.

Milwaukee had a predominately German population, many heavy industries, and a Socialist government by 1910. The new mayor, Emil Seidel, offered some radical suggestions to expand policemen's duties. When he told Janssen that the police should deliver the city's water bill in addition to their other duties, the chief snapped back, "The police force in Milwaukee at the present time is required to do more work outside its regular police duties than any other force in the country." Seidel wanted patrolmen to deliver all the city's mail, deliver election notices, report electric or gas lights not burning, report defective sidewalks, and bring in election returns. They were also expected to take care of dead animals and carcasses found in the streets, patrol the harbor, serve papers for courts and juries, and check peddler and contractor licenses.

Policemen worked 7 days a week and had only 10 vacation days each year. When the Milwaukee Common Council wanted to grant them a day off, Janssen strongly opposed the idea, arguing, "They'd only go from saloon to saloon and booze it up and not be able to report for duty." Police supporters considered this an astonishing slander. Janssen also argued that no other large city gave its men days off. Fortunately, policemen were eventually given a 24-hour day off every two weeks, overriding the objections.

An assassination attempt on former president Theodore Roosevelt's life occurred on October 14, 1912. The act rocked the very foundations of law and order in the city. Roosevelt was shot after dining at the Hotel Gilpatrick by a deranged saloonkeeper named John Schrank, who had followed him to Milwaukee.

The greatest loss of life in U.S. police history, prior to the September 11, 2001, attacks, occurred on November 24, 1917. It was the most tragic day in the history of the MPD. Nine officers and two civilians died in a horrific, destructive blast. A box containing a bomb constructed with a gas pipe and explosive chemicals was discovered at a church. Two boys carried the device to the nearby Central Station, where it exploded hours later while officers were examining it. There was a strong suspicion that anarchists planted the bomb. Suspects were rounded up; however, the case was never solved.

Jacob G. Laubenheimer Jr. became chief in 1921. Shortly thereafter, he attracted national attention with such innovations as the country's first police training school, a traffic bureau, and a bureau of identification. He also reorganized the Detective Bureau and established the Medical Bureau for first aid instruction. The chief increased police service with automobile theft squads, organized the mounted patrolmen and a police boat, and bolstered the department's strength to 705 by 1925.

During Prohibition, the department acquired high-powered rifles, machine guns, and even armored squad cars. The chief's public refusal to tolerate any "disruptive characters" resulted in an underworld warning, "stay away from Milwaukee".

Laubenheimer insisted that department appointments and promotions should be based on merit. Hiring practices were changed. The first two policewomen, Mabel E. Lorch and Mary E. Smith, were hired on November 23, 1922. They were made acting detectives and worked on the morals squad. The first African American patrolman was hired in 1924.

Joseph T. Kluchesky became chief in the midst of the Great Depression (1936) and remained in office throughout World War II. Kluchesky developed one of the best civil defense programs in the country. He demanded citizens be treated honestly and fairly and that all laws be strictly enforced, which probably contributed to Milwaukee's low rate of 1.3 homicides per 100,000 people.

Kluchesky resigned in 1945, and John W. Polcyn was promoted to chief of police. He accelerated the pace of modernization within the department with groundbreaking and radical changes. Polcyn established the Youth Aid Bureau, one of the first in the country. He began one-man squad patrols, combination squad/ambulances, and a 40-hour workweek. Polcyn created the night parking fee system, the first of its kind in the nation. He started the Police Aide Program (1952) in tandem with a program promoting better race relations.

Howard O. Johnson was a 23-year veteran of the MPD and an early-shift commander when he was promoted to chief in 1957. Under Johnson's administration, the Underwater Investigation Unit and Harbor Patrol were established. Johnson modernized the department's tabulating system, established the "roving" patrol wagon, and developed a standardized traffic accident form that was eventually instituted statewide.

When Johnson retired in 1964, Inspector Harold A. Breier, was appointed chief. Five years later, the MPD had 2,256 members, and the city's population was over 800,000. The cooperation of citizens was important to Breier. He often credited citizens with helping to maintain Milwaukee's low crime rate.

Breier experienced serious challenges when violence broke out in the streets of the city in July 1967. In response, he created the Tactical Enforcement Unit, the oldest SWAT team in the nation, which continues to serve today.

In 1971, the Police Administration Building was opened at 749 West State Street. The old police training school moved into new headquarters in 1972 and became known as the Milwaukee Police Safety Academy. The first female "patrolman" was appointed in 1975. Subsequently, patrolmen were referred to as police officers. An exciting time of diversification followed, with significant improvements in radio and communications systems.

Robert J. Ziarnik replaced the retiring Breier in 1984. Technical equipment acquired during this time included a YAG laser for latent fingerprint recovery, the first Automated Fingerprint Identification System (AFIS) in Wisconsin, telecommunications devices for the deaf (TDDs), and the first personal computers. Squad cars were redesigned. During Ziarnik's tenure, officers' uniform design and material were upgraded from wool to cotton and nylon. The MPD was recognized nationally as the best-dressed department of its size in the country.

In the last 20 years, Milwaukee had its first Hispanic, African American, and female chiefs. Philip Arreola, of Hispanic heritage, became chief in November 1989. He emphasized the importance of formal education in the efficient administration of law enforcement. He also advocated community-oriented policing and promoted stronger relationships between officers and citizens. During Arreola's tenure, the well-publicized arrest of serial killer Jeffrey Dahmer, in 1991, catapulted the MPD into the international spotlight. The case was handled capably with the steady, reliable, everyday police work that has made Milwaukee renowned.

Arthur L. Jones became the city's first African American chief on November 15, 1996. He implemented an initiative that focused the department's resources on reducing crime and placed greater accountability on all members. During Jones's term, computers and advanced technology were implemented in crime analysis.

Nannette H. Hegerty was sworn in as Milwaukee's 16th chief on November 18, 2003. She is one of only a few women to head a major metropolitan police department.

Although a definitive history of the MPD exceeds the capacity and scope of this book, a compelling overview of this rich history is presented in the following pages.

One

Before 1901

The first police department in Milwaukee was organized 19 years before the first full-time fire department. William Beck had past law enforcement experience and a rather colorful past before becoming chief. He was a policeman in New York City at age 19. Afterward he mined gold in California, was wounded and captured by Native Americans, was shipwrecked in the Pacific, visited Hawaii, crossed the Isthmus of Panama, and lived in the wilds of Cuba, all before settling down in the "untamed" city of Milwaukee. Beck famously told his men, "It's always necessary to whip a man in a fair fight before you arrest him."

The first seven policeman were Fred Kessler, John Hardy, George Fisher, James Rice, Lawrence S. Ryan, William Garlic, and James M. Smith. According to the 1860 United States Federal Census, Rice was an Irishman born about 1823, living in the Third Ward. John Hardy was born in England about 1827, and William Garlic was born about 1824 in New York. They lived in the Fourth Ward. James Rice drowned on September 8, 1860, in the tragic *Lady Elgin* disaster on Lake Michigan. By 1880, all the original patrolmen were dead except Ryan.

The police department evolved into an efficient, military-style organization by the end of the 19th century. Chief John T. Janssen became known as "the Czar" for his strict enforcement of the law and department rules. Some praised him as a shrewd and clever chief, while others called for him to be "dethroned as an autocrat."

Janssen was president of the National Association of Chiefs in 1898. When over 150 police chiefs from major cities in the United States and Canada gathered in Milwaukee to attend the annual convention, Janssen made a startling suggestion. He proposed that all state penitentiaries be abolished (with a few exceptions for short-term convicts) and that the Philippine Islands be made a penal colony of the United States.

Chief William Beck (1855–October 1861; 1863–1878; 1880–1882). William Beck was born in Stuttgart, Württemberg, Germany, on April 16, 1823, immigrated to the United States in 1828, and settled in Granville, Wisconsin, in 1844. Appointed Milwaukee's first chief of police in September 1855, he served three nonconsecutive terms, being relieved of duty and/or reappointed each time, depending on the presiding mayor. The chief was wounded on the job twice, in 1864 and again in 1872. Beck died on September 8, 1911. (Courtesy of the Milwaukee Police Department.)

"Beck's Badge." This finely crafted, ornate gold star is one of the department's prize possessions. It is the first chief's star, referred to as "Beck's badge." It has an unusual eight points, which was considered lucky by some. In contrast, Chief Robert Wason's badge later had only five. Patrolmen wore six-pointed star badges. Beck's men presented him with a gold-tipped cane. Both the star and cane are prominently displayed at the Milwaukee Police Safety Academy.

CHIEF WALTER SHELDON JOHNSON (OCTOBER 1861–APRIL 1862). Col. Walter Sheldon Johnson (also Johnston) was Milwaukee's second chief. No known likeness of him was displayed until this portrait was discovered in 2007. The son of Austin and Maria Sheldon Johnson, Walter was born on July 12, 1817, in Middlebury, Vermont, where he became a merchant. He married Electra Hagar, and they had one son, Edward. Johnson died on July 6, 1888. (Courtesy of the Henry Sheldon Museum, Middlebury, Vermont.)

CHIEF HERMAN L. PAGE (1862–1863). Herman L. Page was born in Oneida County, New York, on May 27, 1818. He moved to Milwaukee in 1844 and opened a dry goods store. He was a distinguished detective in 1851, and later he accepted the position as undersheriff. Page was elected mayor in 1859. During his tenure as chief, he increased the efficiency of the police force. Page died in Dresden, Germany, in October 1873. (Courtesy of the Milwaukee Police Department.)

Chief Daniel Kennedy (1878–1880). Mayor John Black appointed Daniel Kennedy, an Irishman from Killarney, as chief. Kennedy had served as a roundsman under William Beck. Roundsmen marched out with their men in the evening and placed each on his proper beat. From then until morning, they exercised general supervision over them. They were one rank above patrolman and earned $5 more per month. (Courtesy of the Milwaukee Police Department.)

Oldest Photograph? This is most likely the oldest extant photograph of the department. Unfortunately, the grouping of policemen and city officials cannot be precisely dated. Note that the men are not wearing stars and their hats and jackets are mismatched. Uniform dress for patrolmen, with the exception of roundsmen and detectives, was adopted sometime between 1859 and 1874. (Courtesy of William E. Gielow.)

CENTRAL POLICE STATION. When the old facility located on Broadway and Mason Streets was deemed inadequate in 1880, the Milwaukee Common Council purchased a lot on Oneida Street (East Wells Street) and North Broadway at a cost of $12,000. A new Central Station, designed by Milwaukee architect Henry C. Koch, was opened on March 10, 1885. The building in the foreground was red and housed the police. This photograph shows the station in 1924.

PATROL WAGON, 1893. This vehicle was headquartered at the Central (East Side) Station, which received all reports and calls for patrol wagons. Before the police had their own vehicles, patrolmen carried prisoners, particularly drunks, to jail on their backs, or if available, they used wheelbarrows, carts, or express wagons. The injured were also brought to this station, which was used as an emergency hospital until around 1894. (*Glimpses of Milwaukee.*)

West Side Station (Third Precinct). This brick station, which opened in August 1878, was located on West Walnut Street, between Sixth and Seventh Streets. The first commander was Sgt. John Dunct. The layout was similar to the South Side Station. The office was on the lower floor, and cells with five compartments were in the rear. The station keeper's room was located above the office. In January 1881, the city's police force was divided between the Central, South, and West Side Stations, with the latter being assigned 26 officers. This is the earliest known photograph of a horse-drawn police vehicle. The wagon displays a five-pointed star with a number three inside. A permanent station was constructed on West Galena Street between North Ninth and North Tenth Streets and opened in 1886, which is probably when the group of coppers pictured below assembled for the photograph.

OUT FOR A SLEIGH RIDE, 1893. This sleigh was housed at the West Side Station. Notice the runners that made it ideal for negotiating slippery, snow-clad Milwaukee streets. The winter of 1888 was particularly brutal and may have prompted this utilitarian design. (*Glimpses of Milwaukee.*)

NICHOLAS WEBER. A patrolman at the South Side Station, Nicholas Weber was born on October 25, 1843, in Franklin, Wisconsin. He was a cooper before he enlisted in the Union army. During an interview in 1895, he recalled, "Of twenty-five men who served with me in 1870, I am the only one who is still on the force. All the others are either dead or no longer in Milwaukee." (Courtesy of the Milwaukee County Historical Society.)

CHIEF ROBERT WASON (1882–1884). Robert Wason (also spelled Wasson) was appointed chief of police in 1882 and served until 1884. Wason had served as a deputy sheriff in 1856, and in 1858, he is listed as both deputy and coroner. He was born on May 24, 1817, in Belfast, Ireland, married Pauline Thoss in 1844, and died in the town of Granville on September 18, 1887. His signature appears on this portrait. The police alarm system was established in 1883.

CHIEF LEMUEL (LEM) ELLSWORTH (1884–1885). Lemuel Ellsworth was born in Esopus, Ulster County, New York, on December 27, 1836. He moved to Milwaukee in 1857, where he was engaged in shipbuilding. After one year as chief, he resigned amid allegations he had illegally accepted money. He married Nellie Jones, and they had four children. He died on September 5, 1898, and is buried in historic Forest Home Cemetery on Milwaukee's south side. (Courtesy of the Milwaukee Police Department.)

CHIEF FLORIAN J. RIES (1885–1888). Florian J. Ries was born in Baden, Germany, on April 30, 1843, and immigrated to the United States in 1851. He was a cooper, distinguished Civil War veteran, assemblyman, alderman, and justice of the peace. During his term as chief, Ries was described as being capable and efficient; however, he was eventually fired. The force consisted of about 125 men at the time. Ries was married with seven children. He died in 1910.

BROTHERS ON THE JOB. The men in this photograph are Frank Miller and Anton Falsch. Patrolmen were assigned beats that were considered long enough to keep a man on a "steady walk from the time he started until morning." They reported in on some 100 call boxes during their shift. Patrolmen had to "pull the hook," or lever, at each from a designated spot every two hours. (Courtesy of the Milwaukee County Historical Society.)

CHIEF JOHN T. JANSSEN (1888–1921). John T. Janssen was the first chief appointed by the Fire and Police Commission who had life tenure. He immigrated in 1861 and joined the department in 1877. In his early years, he was known as a fearless officer. When Janssen retired in April 1921, the *Milwaukee Sentinel* reported, "No figure in Milwaukee history has been the focal point of so much controversy as Chief Janssen." He died three years later. (Courtesy of the Milwaukee Police Department.)

BERGES'S MEN. This photograph, likely taken sometime before 1900, shows Lt. Joseph Berges and fellow officers on the steps of the old courthouse. Berges, sergeant at the West Side Station in 1881, was a native Prussian. He came to Wisconsin in 1842 and settled in Milwaukee in 1859. He was a Civil War veteran and the father of one child. Old-time members of the department Sergeant Kranich and F. A. Miller are also in the picture.

SECOND PRECINCT STATION (SOUTH SIDE STATION). The south side of Milwaukee was a rough area and home to many tough and rowdy characters. The demand for a police station on that side of town was long and persistent. Opened on October 28, 1891, this two-story brick and stone station, described as handsome at the time, and garage was built on the corner of First Avenue and Mineral Street (later South Sixth and West Mineral Streets) at a slightly higher cost than other stations—about $30,000. It was heated with steam and had running water and electric lighting throughout. The basement had two rows of cells, one having 16, the other 12. The first floor accommodated the general office with the station keeper's desk and a vault. There were also quarters for two horses and the patrol wagon. The basement had room for 12 horses.

THE PATROLMEN'S ROOM.

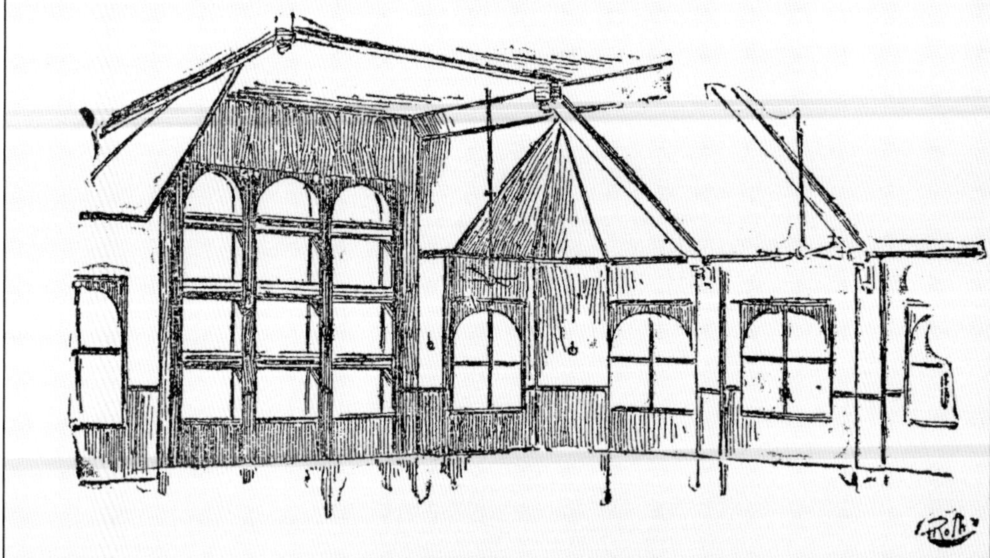

THE FUTURE GYMNASIUM.

STATION INTERIOR. These sketches of the interior of the South Side Station illustrate the gymnasium on the second floor and a sleeping apartment for patrolmen. A hayloft could be used to store almost four tons. Sgt. Garrett Green and roundsman Louis E. Wallerman commanded the force there. Four officers did post duty. There were 9 day patrolmen and 18 night patrolmen. After the station opened, the police reported a 25 percent drop in arrests and disorders in the area. Interestingly, the first police department rule book (1890) established emergency shelters in local police stations to give aid and comfort to the homeless and destitute. The new Second Precinct Station opened to help with the load. On any given night, 50 to 75 "lodgers" were accommodated in the stations' so-called tramp rooms in the early days. This practice was continued until the early 1960s.

FRONT OF THE OLD COURTHOUSE. Milwaukee's second courthouse was located at Jefferson and Jackson Streets, across from St. John's Cathedral. Note the old hitching post and the wooden footbridge spanning the brick road. By 1893, the force consisted of the chief, an inspector, a captain, 3 lieutenants, 3 sergeants, 8 roundsmen, 10 detectives, 225 patrolmen, a secretary, a matron, a superintendent of police alarm telegraph, 8 station keepers, 2 linemen, and a batteryman.

SHOOTISTS, 1896. These 10 serious-looking policemen with mustaches were crack rifle shots and members of the MPD. Together they organized the Stevens Rifle Club. The department attracted some of the finest marksmen. Accurate shooting was an advantage to the men professionally, and many engaged in competitive events in their off-duty time. Policemen have been awarded many sharpshooting titles throughout the years. (Courtesy of Journal Sentinel, Inc., reproduced with permission.)

POLICE MATRON. The first female employee in the MPD was likely Mary Buchanan, who was appointed matron in 1883. She was succeeded by Nellie Milbrath, wife of the janitor at the station. Forced to leave when her husband resigned, Milbrath was replaced by Susan Kluppak in 1890. All female prisoners were in her custody. It was reported that Kluppak believed in treating all prisoners in her care with as much kindness as possible and tried to make the station homelike for them. She was charged with searching the women before placing them in a cell. Her other duties included looking after the station laundry and making sure the policemen's sleeping compartments were kept in good condition. She occupied two rooms at the Central Station, where she provided her own meals. When this sketch of Kluppak appeared in the newspaper in January 1896, her salary was $25 per month. She was on constant call and was required to be on hand to receive female prisoners at all hours of the day or night.

Drill Squads, 1896. One hour of each day during the week, except Sundays and Mondays, was devoted to drilling. This photograph of some dandy coppers, members of the Wednesday drill squad, (above) contains the names of the 38 men shown here on the steps of the courthouse. One of the ways early police commissioners exercised their oversight responsibility was to request yearly full-dress inspections of the fire and police departments. On the appointed date, departments would muster in full-dress uniform and perform various military-style drills and marching maneuvers. They presented a very credible appearance at inspections before the mayor, commissioners, city officials, and the general public, who reviewed them. The Saturday drill squad is pictured below.

INSPECTION. Referred to as the "March of Bluecoats," 250 members of the police department make their way from the Broadway Street station to city hall square in this photograph by A. A. Hills, titled "Milwaukee Police Inspection, October 26, 1898." On this afternoon, the men were inspected by Mayor David S. Rose, the Fire and Police Commission, other city officials, and about 2,000 spectators. A Milwaukee Police Band concert followed the inspection. This was the ribbon worn by Chief John T. Janssen at the National Association of Chiefs, convened the same day.

BEAT COP. Patrolman William Leuenberg from Central Station (No. 1) looks particularly handsome in his pot hat. (Courtesy of the Milwaukee County Historical Society.)

DRESS UNIFORM. This full-length view of an officer clearly shows his stick, full coat, and belt, which was very heavy. The frock coat had 16 buttons, and the white collar was sharp and stiff and cut into the neck.

MILWAUKEE POLICE BAND, 1898. A group of policemen who were proficient whistlers got together to practice at the old Second Precinct Station in the fall of 1897. They found they liked to entertain and discovered that many of them had musical talents. Officer William Stupenagel, who had a musical background, organized several men into a small band. Chief John T. Janssen was pleased, and he gave the group official status as the Milwaukee Police Band. On April 9, 1898, the band first performed before members of the department playing "Yankee Doodle," "The Star-Spangled Banner," and "El Capitan." In 1922, they made an appearance with John Philip Sousa and played his march "Gallant Seventh." In 1926, they were honored with their own tune. "The Milwaukee Police Band March" was written by Howard B. Weeks, a native Californian who moved to Milwaukee. The original manuscript is housed in the MPD library at the Milwaukee Police Safety Academy. The Milwaukee Police Band is still active today, performing at a variety of local, state, and national events, including the Special Olympics, memorials, concerts, and parades.

Two

FROM 1901 TO 1919

A new badge was only one of many changes. Two new stations were built in the fourth and fifth districts. The chief instituted reforms aimed at improving efficiency and discipline. These included improvements in communications, the acquisition of motorcycles and motorized vehicles, and a new-style uniform. Some of his policies and actions were highly controversial.

In March 1911, the City of Milwaukee installed the first call boxes, which replaced the kiosks of olden days. Each box contained three separate compartments. One was for regular fire alarms, the second for police telephones, and the third for general use.

A serious rift between Chief John T. Janssen and his men occurred when new uniforms for patrolmen were mandated. Five policemen lost their jobs protesting the cost of the new overcoats, which they had to bear themselves.

Automaker Henry Ford reportedly once said, "You can have a car in any color you want, as long as it is black." All early police vehicles were black, except ambulances. The first motorized squad car was introduced in 1913. It was equipped with lamps on the right and left sides etched with *1913*. The car also had a banner imprinted with *Milwaukee* on it, and there was a squeeze bulb horn. By 1914, all horse-drawn patrol wagons in the MPD were replaced by motorized vehicles.

New ambulances went into service in February 1917. One was kept at the Central Station, the other on the south side. Previously the South Side Station used a patrol wagon to convey patients. The ambulances were maroon in color and outfitted with electric heat and all the modern accessories of the age. Joseph "Doc" Johnson called the new vehicle a splendid new "palace car for the sick."

In 1917, the MPD suffered the most costly explosion in police history. Nine officers lost their lives. They were detectives Fred W. Kaiser, David G. O'Brien, Stephen Stecker, Charles Seehawer, Albert Templin, and Paul J. Weiler, plainclothes officer Frank M. Caswin, night station keeper Henry J. Deckert, and alarm operator Edward Spindler. Edward Spindler's 90-year-old widow, Ella Spindler, was still collecting a paltry widow's pension of $35 per month in 1973. Detectives Louis Hartmand and Herman Bergin were seriously injured.

CHARLES HENKE. Patrolman Charles Henke (star No. 325) was assigned to the Third Precinct Station. He resided in the Ninth Ward with his wife, Annie, and their three children. He was about 33 years old when this photograph was taken in 1900. (Courtesy of the Milwaukee County Historical Society.)

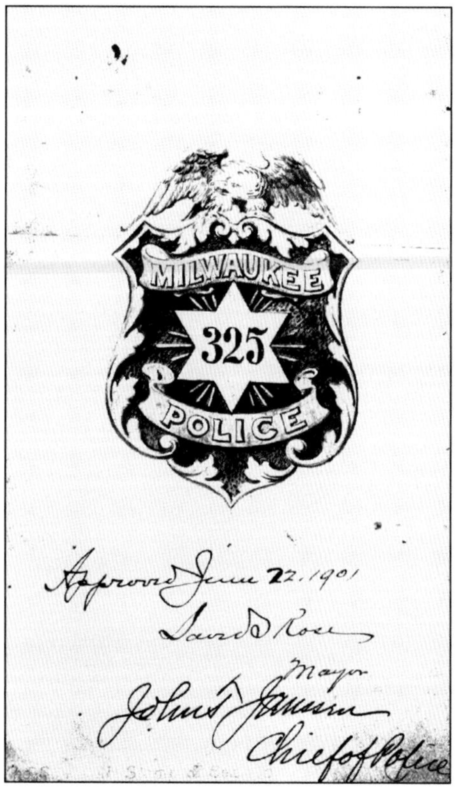

BADGE PROTOTYPE. This original sketch of the new design received the approval of Milwaukee's mayor David S. Rose and chief of police John T. Janssen, whose signatures appear on the drawing, dated June 22, 1901. The design incorporates a six-pointed star, which has the same number as the star worn by Charles Henke in 1900. The new badge symbolized the beginning of a new era in the department.

JAMES SHERIDAN. First Precinct Central Station (East Side) officer James Sheridan poses for a formal portrait with his new badge. The regulation belt and baton are also clearly visible.

TOP BUTTON DONE. The men in this photograph are members of the Third Precinct Station. Dress regulations specified that only the top button of the policemen's uniforms had to be buttoned to pass inspection. Many veterans put on weight over the years but could not afford to buy new uniforms, which were purchased at their own expense.

Night Detail. This photograph shows the men assigned to night duty at the Central Station in 1902. That year, there were 320 men on the force.

Opening Fourth Precinct, 1904. This group photograph is dated May 2, 1904. Paul Gurda, pictured in one of the cameos, was the great-uncle of well-known Milwaukee historian John Gurda. Paul began his career at the Bay View Station, rose to sergeant in 1920, then to lieutenant, and transferred to the Sixth District Station when it opened. He rose finally to captain in 1938 and retired in 1944, after 40 years with the MPD.

Fourth District Station (Bay View Station). The new Fourth District Station was located on the east side of South Allis Street between East Lincoln and East Bay Streets in the 10th Ward. It consisted of a two-story brick station, two-story brick office, one-story brick and concrete cell room, and one-story brick and reinforced concrete fireproof garage. Construction costs were approximately $34,000. This photograph is dated 1928.

FIFTH DISTRICT STATION. This station was located at North Third and West Hadley Streets. Virtually identical to the Fourth District Station, it was built the same year. The lieutenant's office was located behind the big window. The captain's office was on the right, and the switchboard (the North Side Board) was on the second floor. The South Side Board was located in the Second District Station.

POLICE WAGON, 1905. This patrol wagon from the Central Station was photographed in front of the Fifth Precinct Station, where there was room for an ambulance and patrol wagon. The driver is John Settgast. Charles Bock is on the left, and Herman Marquart is on the right. (Courtesy Journal Sentinel, Inc., reproduced with permission.)

COMMISSIONER. The Fire and Police Commission, the oldest civil service authority in Wisconsin, was established in 1885. It was responsible for setting employment standards, testing candidates, and appointing both the police and fire chief. This caricature, from a rare edition of *Milwaukeeans as We See 'Em* (1904), depicts longtime commissioner John F. Burnham, president of Burnham Brick and Supply Company, wearing two hats. (Author's collection.)

FIRST AMBULANCE. Police ambulance service began in November 1907. This vehicle, drawn by one horse, was the pride of the department. Early driver Joseph "Doc" Johnson was appointed to the force on November 8, 1888. The police provided first aid services and conveyance to the Milwaukee County General Hospital. Due to rough pavement, the ambulance suffered much wear and tear over the years.

NIGHT DETAIL. This portrait of the members of the night detail of the Third Precinct was taken in 1907. Group photographs, like this one, were taken at uneven intervals in later years, but few survive today.

"FLYING SQUAD," 1909. The so-called flying squad assembles in Lt. Frank Miller's office at the Central Station. From left to right are detectives John Hammes and Miller (seated) and detectives Edward Biersach, Harry McCrory, and Paul Pergande. This term was applied to specific officers, usually detectives, who were assigned to station house duty until a crime was reported. Then they "flew" to the crime scene to investigate the situation.

POST DUTY, 1909. This photograph was taken at Third Street and Wisconsin (formerly Grand) Avenue, then the city's busiest intersection. Heavy wagons driven by careless drivers were considered a public menace, as were reckless motormen. Automobiles traveled about 12 miles per hour, and one passed by about once every 15 minutes. Armed with a friendly smile, traffic officer Schultz is ready to cite drivers violating the traffic laws and assist pedestrians. (Courtesy of William E. Gielow.)

DEPARTMENT'S FIRST MOTORCYCLE. Sgt. Fergus McKenney sits on top of the first motorcycle used by the MPD in 1910. It was manufactured by Thor, a company located in Aurora, Illinois. The motorcycle patrol was established three years before, when one motorcycle was purchased. Two more were added the next year. Early riders were not required to wear uniforms, protective gear, or helmets. (Courtesy of the Milwaukee County Historical Society.)

BASEBALL, 1911. This photograph, taken on July 8, 1911, captures some athletic members of the MPD who formed a baseball team. They played at the old Brewer Ball Park.

Bodyguards and Assassination Attempt. The officers assigned to protect Pres. William Howard Taft during his Milwaukee visit in 1911 are, from left to right, Frank Conway, Fergus McKenney, Dan Kugler, and G. Goodman. The two motorcycles shown on the left are Thors; the two on the right are Harley-Davidsons, with battery ignitions. They were probably about one year old. Each was equipped with speedometers, and their top speed was around 50 miles per hour. Former president Theodore Roosevelt is seen below leaving the train station, before the attempt on his life, one year earlier. He was scheduled to deliver a speech at the auditorium in the evening. His assailant, John Schrank, was captured by Sgt. Albert Murray, an Irishman, who was assisted by several other officers. It was a most important arrest for the MPD. Schrank was quickly tried and sent to the Northern Hospital for the Insane at Oshkosh a few months later. Pictured here, from left to right, are police sergeant Robert Flood, newsboy Howard Cunningham, Gov. George W. Peck, Roosevelt, press club representative Oliver Remey, and Frank Cannon. (Above, courtesy of the Milwaukee County Historical Society; below, courtesy of the Wisconsin Historical Society, Image ID 20916.)

NEW UNIFORMS. Daniel O'Loughlin (left) and Tom Johnston, Milwaukee's first traffic officer, are seen at the corner of North Plankinton and West Wisconsin Avenues on February 26, 1914. Johnston wears the new-style overcoat. Longer than the previous coat, it had a big, roll collar and fewer buttons. Patrolmen often referred to them as "horse blankets" because they were all weight and no warmth. The new buttons were impressed with the seal of the state of Wisconsin. (Courtesy of the Milwaukee County Historical Society.)

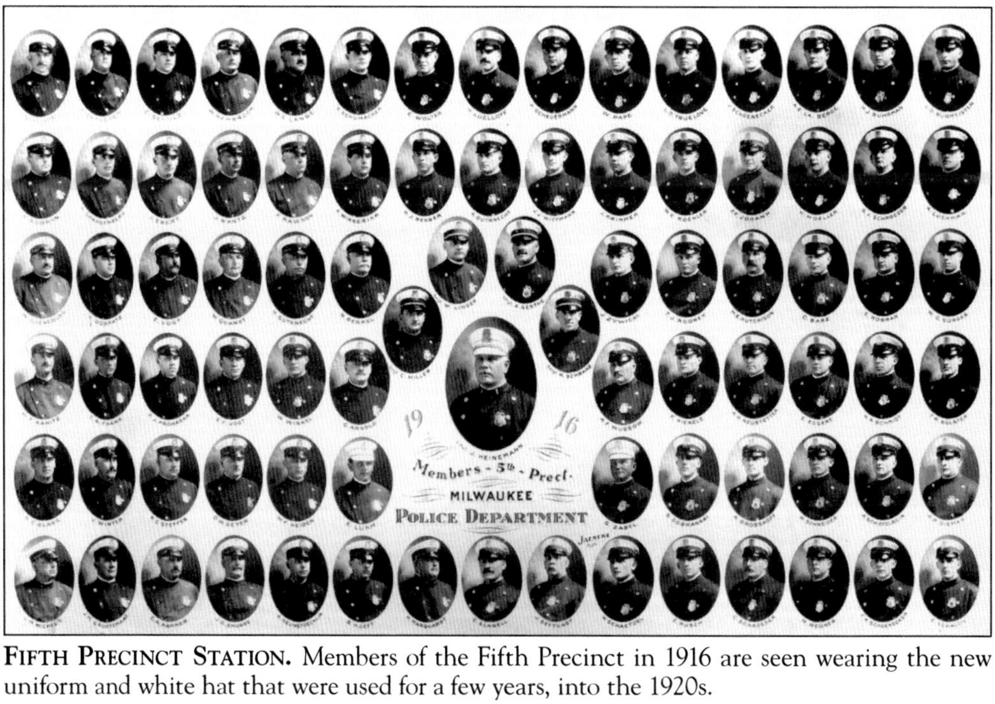

FIFTH PRECINCT STATION. Members of the Fifth Precinct in 1916 are seen wearing the new uniform and white hat that were used for a few years, into the 1920s.

Part 1

THE SUNDAY SENTINEL

LATEST EDITION

70,452

MILWAUKEE, SUNDAY MORNING, NOVEMBER 25, 1917—EIGHTY-TWO PAGES

PRICE FIVE CENTS

NARCHIST'S BOMB EXPLODES IN POLICE STATION--KILLS ELEVEN

Section of Central Police Station Where Eleven Met Their Death

NINE OFFICERS AND 2 OTHERS ARE VICTIMS

Detectives Are Hurled to Death Examining Explosive Brought From Third Ward.

MANGLED BODIES ARE HARD TO IDENTIFY

Two Policemen Injured in Blast While Many Others Miraculously Escape Tragedy's Toll.

VICTIMS OF BOMB

THE DEAD.

CHARLES SEEHAUER, 1172 Richards street; detective.
STEPHEN STECKER, 623 Center street; detective.
DAVID G. O'BRIEN, 166 Prospect avenue; detective.
FRED W. KAISER, 549 Farwell avenue; detective.
PAUL J. WEILER, 556 Twenty-seventh avenue; detective.
EDWARD SPINDLER, 2919 Walnut street, operator.
ALBERT TEMPLIN, 518 Madison street; detective.
FRANK M. CASWIN, 159 Eighteenth street; plain clothesman.
HENRY DECKERT, 117 Sheridan Lane; night station keeper.
MISS CATHERINE WALKER, 434 Sixth street.
UNIDENTIFIED ITALIAN.

THE INJURED:

LOUIS A. HARTMAN, 3012 Cherry street; detective; compound fracture of arm and slugs in legs. Probably will recover.
HERMAN BERGIN, 1679 Seventh street; detective; severe flesh wounds and injuries to head. Will recover.

25 MEN ARRESTED IN BIG ROUNDUP

Capt. John Sullivan Puts Squad of Fifty at Work on Explosion.

WILL ROOT OUT I. W. W.

"Suspects to Be Grilled as They Have Never Been Before."

REMAINS ARE TAKEN TO FUNERAL PARLOR

BOMB MEANT FOR PASTOR AND FLOCK

Maude Richter, Social Settlement Worker, Tells of Finding Death Device.

TO EXPLODE AS CROWD WAS GREATEST

Few Anarchists Hated Rev. August Juliana for Causing Recent Arrests.

DETECTIVE'S WATCH BLOWN FROM POCKET

DECKERT GETS BOMB

HIS WEDDING RING BLOWN FROM FINGER

HAVE NARROW ESCAPES

TIMED TO EXPLODE

BOMB TO STATION

CENTRAL STATION BOMBING. November 24, 1917, was the most tragic day in the history of the MPD. It was the greatest loss of life in U.S. police history, in a single incident, prior to the September 11, 2001, attacks. Nine officers and two civilians, including one woman, were horribly killed in a destructive blast that occurred at 7:30 p.m., just after roll call. The explosion heavily damaged the assembly room. Many were injured. The bomb was found on Saturday at an Italian church in the Third Ward and was taken to the nearby station where it exploded hours later while officers examined it. The entire city was shocked and disgusted by reports of mangled bodies and property damage. The pastor of the church was the intended victim. There was a strong suspicion that anarchists planted the bomb; however, the case was never solved. (Author's collection.)

New West Side Station (Third Precinct). After the old West Side Station closed, a new two-story brick building with a six-car garage was constructed in 1918 at North Twelfth and West Vine Streets (1747 North Twelfth Street) at a cost of $38,000. The site was later renovated, becoming home to the city's police and fire alarm system. This station closed when the new Third District Station, designed by Charles E. Malig, was opened at 4715 West Vliet Street in September 1937.

Three

The 1920s

The 1920s were roaring, and the MPD was making giant leaps forward, with Jacob G. Laubenheimer Jr. (1874–1936) as chief innovator. He received credit for elevating the city's status from 29th among the 34 major American cities to a reputation of unequaled eminence for quality of police protection, crimelessness, and public order. By mid-decade, the most common offenses in the city were traffic infractions, drunkenness second, and disorderly conduct and dry law violations tied for third. Statistics show that over half of those arrested were single and most were between the ages of 21 and 40. Police reported that Milwaukee's youths, up to the age of 17, were well behaved.

The first policewomen were hired in 1922. They devoted their efforts to the welfare of women and children involved in police cases. It is interesting to note that married women were allowed to apply for the position at a time when most employers required female employees to be single. Judson Walter Minor Jr., an African American, was appointed to the force on October 13, 1924. He was assigned to a beat in the upper Third Ward.

Officers no longer had to rely on their fists to win over hearts and minds but often showed a kinder, gentler nature, as a touching story reported in the *Milwaukee Leader* reveals. In December 1925, veteran traffic officer Emil Heun appeared in court with a 17-year-old boy whom he had arrested on a serious charge. He entered an eloquent plea in the young man's behalf. "Judge, I'll take this boy into my home if you'll put him on probation." As he spoke, he reportedly put his arms around the boy and addressed him directly. "If the judge lets you off, sonny, I'll take you right home to a good old-fashioned German dinner. You'll be our boy to ma and me. Do you want to go?" The boy nodded, with tears in his eyes. Heun had lost his own son two years before and found the yuletide season unbearable without him. The judge granted Heun's request, cautioning the boy never to betray the confidence of the officer. The boy was placed on probation for three years.

CHIEF JACOB G. LAUBENHEIMER JR. (1921–1936). Jacob G. Laubenheimer Jr. was born in Milwaukee on March 19, 1874. He was educated and attended business college in Milwaukee. Laubenheimer worked at the Wisconsin Telephone Company before being appointed secretary stenographer and keeper of saloon license records for the MPD in 1893. He became a patrolman in June 1899, was promoted to detective in 1901, and was appointed chief on May 7, 1921.

THE LAUBENHEIMER FAMILY. This photograph allows a rare glimpse at the chief of police and his family. Most likely taken sometime in the mid-1920s, it shows Jacob G. Laubenheimer Jr. with his wife, Catherine Laubenheimer (née McCormack) and their children, John G. (born around 1914) and Jane (born around 1917). The chief's father, Jacob Sr., joined the force in 1880 and was named assistant chief by John T. Janssen in 1912.

Review. Traffic officers pose on their Harley-Davidson JD motorcycles in front of the Johann Wolfgang von Goethe and Friedrich von Schiller monument in Washington Park in 1921. It was erected by the German citizens of Wisconsin on June 14, 1908, and rededicated in 1960 by Milwaukee's German societies. Goethe is on the left, and Schiller is on the right. The impressive monument still stands today, a short distance from the park's band shell. (Courtesy of the Milwaukee County Historical Society).

Fourth Precinct Station. This group photograph shows the officers assigned to the Fourth Precinct (or South Side Station) under the command of Lt. John F. Wesolowski in 1921. This facility was closed and relocated to Sixty-ninth Street and Silver Spring Drive in 1965.

MILWAUKEE'S FIRST AFRICAN AMERICAN OFFICER. Judson Walter Minor Jr. was born in 1897 in Lee County, Georgia. He moved to Milwaukee in 1918, joined the force in 1924, and resigned in December 1926. His captain said that he had an excellent record, but Minor was upset with the large number of false complaints lodged against him. In 1929, he was working as a crane operator in a steel mill. He and his wife, Hattie Lee Minor (née Thomas), both died in 1981. They are buried in Evergreen Cemetery in Milwaukee.

HARLEY-DAVIDSON. This unidentified officer proudly poses with this Harley-Davidson motorcycle in a photograph taken in 1926. It was capable of speeds of up to 60 miles per hour. Until 1921, motorcycle officers wore civilian clothes. The MPD owned about two dozen motorcycles in 1927. A few years later, a rash of accidents claimed the lives of several motorcycle officers in the city.

Police Patrols. One new and one older model patrol car (wagon) were photographed in front of the Fourth District Station. Slang terms like *paddy wagon* and *Black Maria* were often used to refer to these vehicles, which were used to transport people to the station. The garage boss, traditionally the senior officer on shift, maintained all vehicles and equipment. In the days of the horse-drawn wagons, these caretakers were called wagon bosses. The American Automobile Company in Milwaukee distributed Pierce Arrow patrols to the MPD, which it referred to in its advertisements as "the most efficient police department in the world."

POLICE AMBULANCE NO. 1. The vehicles of the MPD were photographed early in 1926 by Frank Schmidt at the request of Chief Jacob G. Laubenheimer Jr. These photographs show a fine, well-maintained fleet that included Lincolns.

SIXTH DISTRICT STATION. A new brick and concrete police station to serve the southwest side was opened in September 1927 at 3220 West Burnham Street. A crowd of over 2,500 citizens, including Mayor Daniel W. Hoan and other city officials, attended an afternoon dedication ceremony held in front of the garage adjacent to the station. Sixty-six officers and patrolmen were assigned to the station. The first arrest, for drunk and disorderly conduct, occurred three and one-half hours after opening. The office area was to the right of the front door, inside. The lieutenant's office was off to the left. The assembly room was upstairs to the left, and the sergeant's room was on the right (east side). Cells were in the back.

CELL. Cell No. 13, undoubtedly an unlucky number for anyone who occupied it, was located at the Central Police Station. Frank Burns was the sergeant in charge when this photograph was taken on January 4, 1928. Many years later, Chief John W. Polcyn commented to the press that these cells are "comparable to the dungeons of medieval times."

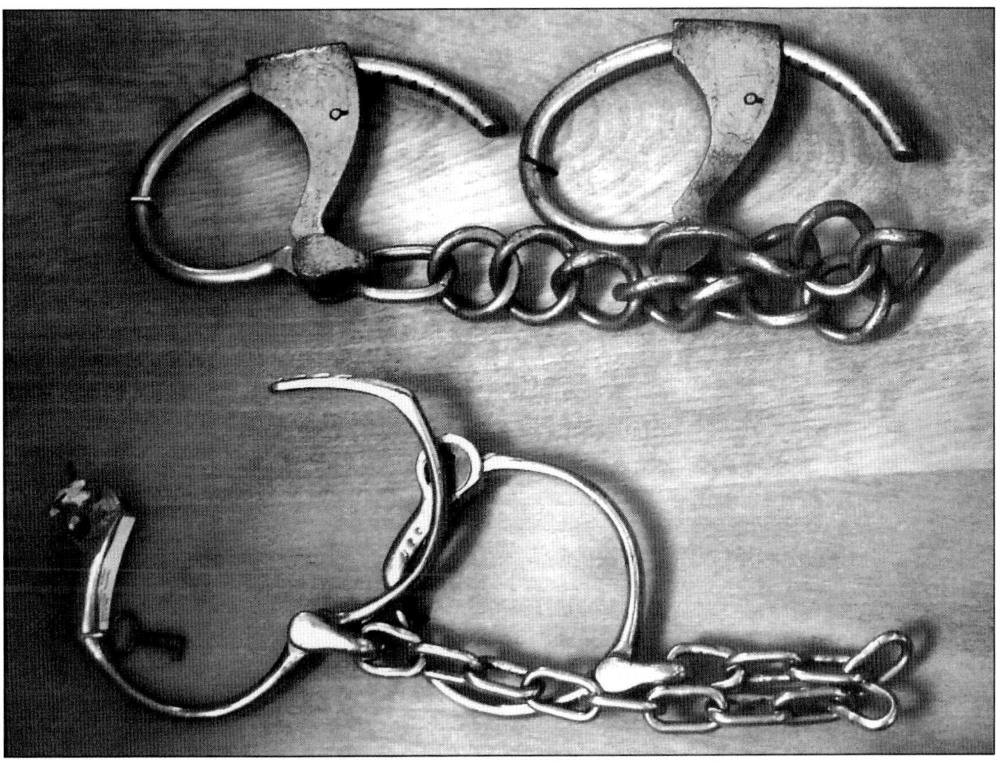

HANDCUFFS. Several curious examples of the oldest handcuffs used in the department are on display in the halls of the Milwaukee Police Safety Academy. They range from very old iron restraints for the wrists and ankles to less cumbersome models. (Author's collection.)

Tommy Guns. The department acquired several Thompson submachine guns (tommy guns) in 1928. Developed in 1920 by Brig. Gen. John T. Thompson, these legendary guns were the weapons of choice of many bootleggers and gangsters because they were more compact and lighter than earlier models. The tommy gun had tremendous firepower, making it easy to hit targets from a distance. Loaded with armor-piercing ammunition, it could penetrate heavy doors.

Firearms Training. Police reported regularly for firearms training at the Milwaukee Gun Club on the lakefront. Officers tested weapons, like the new machine guns, before turning them over to patrolmen. In the course of demonstrating these weapons, advice such as "release the safety catch and let her go" was dispensed. Police were acutely aware of the need to stay one step ahead of the criminals.

PROHIBITION. A policeman dismantles a still. After the country was declared dry in 1919, many citizens continued to brew beer and make wine (within the lawful limits and in the old German tradition) at home to satisfy their own needs. Others ran larger, illegal operations such as the one shown here. (Courtesy of the Milwaukee County Historical Society.)

TRAFFIC OFFICER. Looking dapper, this officer is directing ("swinging") traffic near Herman's Department Store, a Milwaukee landmark. One traffic post man said that it was so cold on his corner in the winter that he had to dance around to keep his feet warm, and it was so windy that he had to put some gravel on the road to stand on so he could keep his footing against the icy blasts.

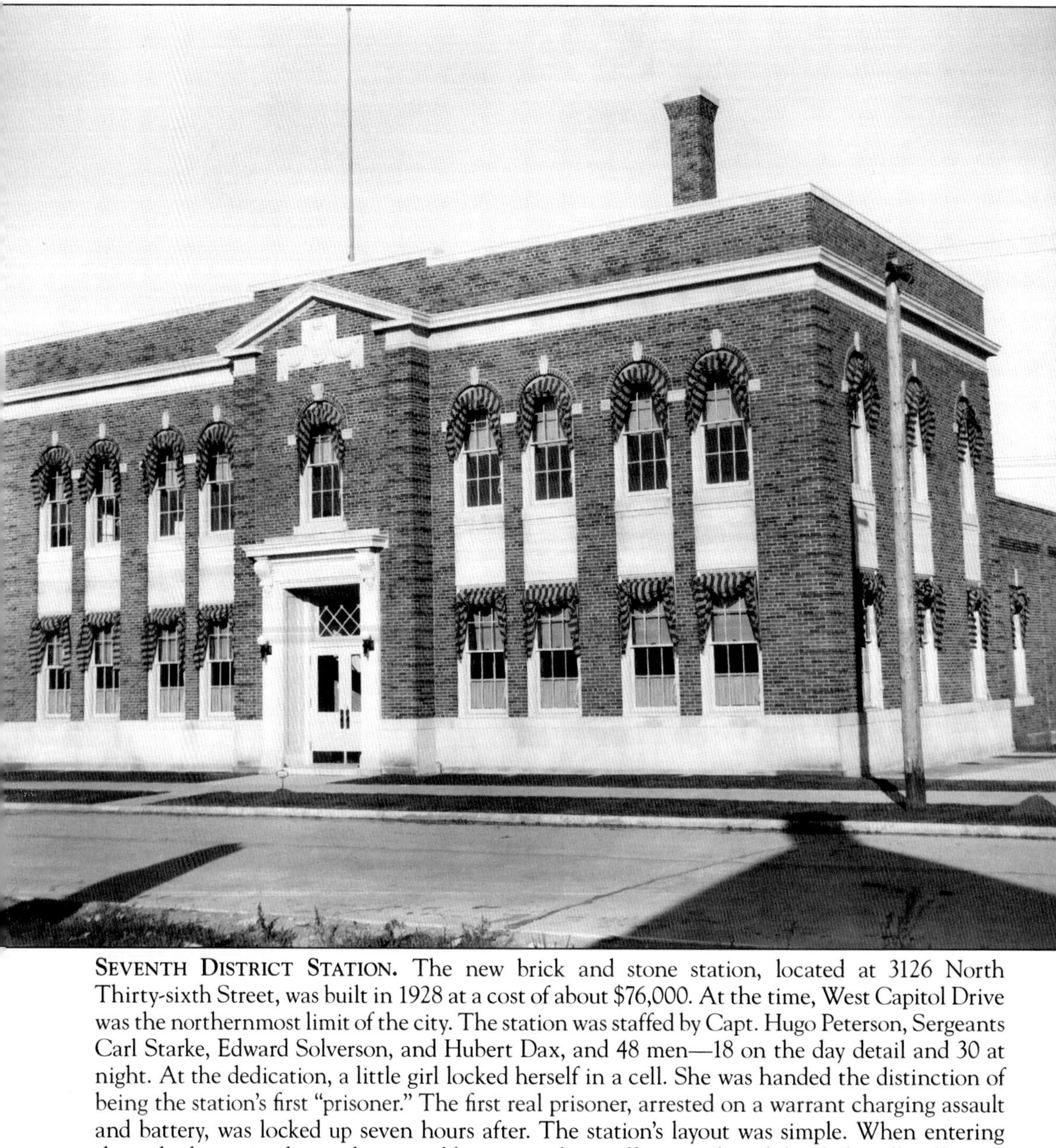

SEVENTH DISTRICT STATION. The new brick and stone station, located at 3126 North Thirty-sixth Street, was built in 1928 at a cost of about $76,000. At the time, West Capitol Drive was the northernmost limit of the city. The station was staffed by Capt. Hugo Peterson, Sergeants Carl Starke, Edward Solverson, and Hubert Dax, and 48 men—18 on the day detail and 30 at night. At the dedication, a little girl locked herself in a cell. She was handed the distinction of being the station's first "prisoner." The first real prisoner, arrested on a warrant charging assault and battery, was locked up seven hours after. The station's layout was simple. When entering through the main doors, the assembly room, where officers gathered for daily roll calls, was located on the right side; to the left, there was a long desk and public reception area, where the desk sergeant presided. The lieutenant's and captain's offices were nearby. Interrogation rooms and the cell block were at the rear of the building. A garage exiting on Auer Avenue was at the end of the L-shaped extension.

Four

The 1930s

Prohibition, which began on July 1, 1919, and ended in 1933, was particularly difficult for Milwaukeeans. When the Volstead Act was passed, some city breweries were already 80 years old. Most survived the duration by retooling their plants and producing soda water, syrups, or near beers. Prohibition also affected the citizenry. There was one tavern for every 230 residents in 1918, and they were all well attended. Racketeers feared the MPD because it strictly enforced the law and adopted a tough stance on organized crime. Gangsters never gained a foothold in Milwaukee, as they had in nearby Chicago.

In 1930, the MPD received good news. The Wickersham Committee, a national commission whose task it was to investigate municipal police corruption, reported to the United States Congress, "Milwaukee is often cited as a city free from crime or where a criminal is speedily detected, arrested, promptly tried and sent on his way to serve time. No other city has this record." It concluded that the MPD was a "national model of corruption-free policing," also citing the "good moral character" of Chief Jacob G. Laubenheimer Jr.

The Great Depression was difficult for everyone. Policemen were happy to have steady jobs in a time when most Americans were unemployed and suffering great hardships; however, this relative security came at a price. City of Milwaukee policemen and firemen "voluntarily" accepted a 10 percent cut in pay, which was supposed to help the city's financial state. The city was having difficulty collecting taxes, and it could not pay out salaries for a four-month period. When salaries resumed, it printed its own money (scrip) and paid officers with it. Only a few merchants took the scrip at full value. Thereafter, the city paid out salaries in one-quarter U.S. dollars and three-quarters scrip. Four to five percent was deducted for pension costs on basis of full pay. A few years later, firemen received a compensatory five days off for their "voluntary" 10 percent donations, but policemen received nothing.

In September 1936, Chief Joseph T. Kluchesky decided to retire the police horses from duty, but they were reinstated by public demand in November that same year.

POLICE TRAINING SCHOOL. Some of the older members of the force sneered at the new police training school when it was established, regarding it as a "finishing school." However, the course of instruction was sound, practical, and tough. Classes included Criminal Law, City Ordinance, Rules and Regulations of the Department, Deportment, Discipline, Evidence and Its Proper Presentation in Court Cases, Observation, First Aid to the Injured, Hygiene, Military Courtesy and Drill, and Revolver and Target Practice. Capt. Floyd McGuire was the first head of the school from 1923 until 1935. Potentially contagious or deadly diseases such as diphtheria, typhoid fever, smallpox, and measles were still serious public health threats in the 1930s. The Public Health Department frequently imposed quarantines, which were enforced by MPD officers, to help control the spread of the diseases.

SIGNS, SIGNS. The traffic signs seen here were finished at the police paint shop, located at 476 Broadway Street in 1930. Nine years earlier, Chief Jacob G. Laubenheimer Jr. initiated the trial installation of "silent policemen" (better known as traffic lights) at downtown intersections. The first was a mechanical stop-and-go signal. By 1922, there were two in the city. Laubenheimer followed New York City's lead in implementing the new technology, and he created the Traffic Bureau in 1921. Three years later, police experimented with a safety island on Kilbourn Avenue, and further traffic regulations were put in place in 1925.

"CALLING ALL CARS." The first radio dispatch call by the MPD was made on Christmas Eve, December 24, 1930. The earliest call logs have been preserved. The first official transmission from the station was "Squad 4 and 13, man shot, 16 and National." One-way (receiver) radios were installed in squad cars the same year, helping police to protect a city of 578,000 people. Wesley J. Wiseman is pictured at the controls.

ALARM OPERATORS. This is the MPD dispatch system (Communications Bureau) as it looked on April 20, 1932. The department utilized the most modern methods of communication at its disposal to combat crime. This once meant using complete radio systems, interconnected telephones, and Teletype machines.

ASSESSING THE DAMAGE. An officer from the Traffic Bureau demonstrates how gunshots damaged the rear window in this vehicle. Although Milwaukee was safer than most cities of its size, it was not immune to crime.

RECRUITMENT. Job applications are distributed to prospective patrolmen in the Safety Building gymnasium early on the morning of May 17, 1933. Applicants had to conform to strict height, weight, and age requirements before joining the force. Prohibition in the United States ended later that year when the Volstead Act (National Prohibition Act of 1919) was repealed on December 5.

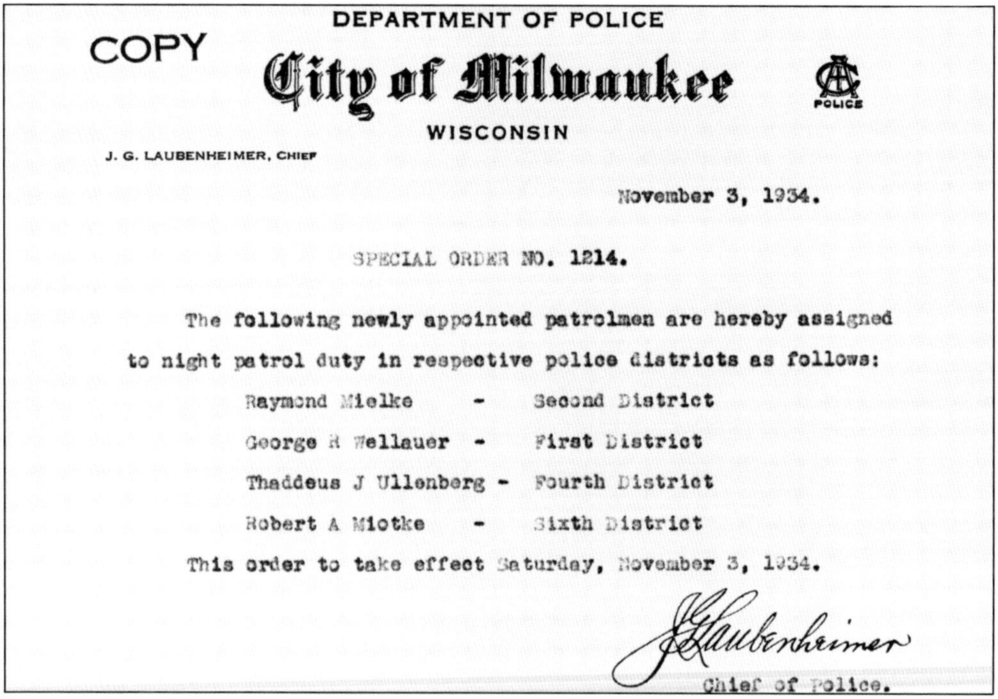

DEPARTMENT OF POLICE

COPY

City of Milwaukee

POLICE

WISCONSIN

J. G. LAUBENHEIMER, CHIEF

November 3, 1934.

SPECIAL ORDER NO. 1214.

The following newly appointed patrolmen are hereby assigned to night patrol duty in respective police districts as follows:

Raymond Mielke - Second District

George R Wellauer - First District

Thaddeus J Ullenberg - Fourth District

Robert A Miotke - Sixth District

This order to take effect Saturday, November 3, 1934.

J G Laubenheimer

Chief of Police.

SPECIAL ORDER NO. 1214. This letter, signed by Chief Jacob G. Laubenheimer Jr., confirms the appointment and assignments of four new patrolmen in November 1934: George R. Wellauer, who served for 27 years, under four chiefs; Thaddeus J. Ullenberg, who become a detective and served 38 years and 4 months, until his death in 1973; and Sgt. Robert A. Miotke, who died in December 1995. Nothing is known about Raymond Mielke. (Author's collection).

NEW PATROLMAN. Milwaukee policemen were required to reside within the city limits, a practice continued to this day. A proud mother, Mary Ella Wellauer photographed her son, George, in his summer uniform at their home on North Fifty-fifth Street in 1935. He worked out of the First District Station, 935 North Eighth Street, as a patrolman and acting detective (in 1944) until he was transferred to District Seven. (Author's collection).

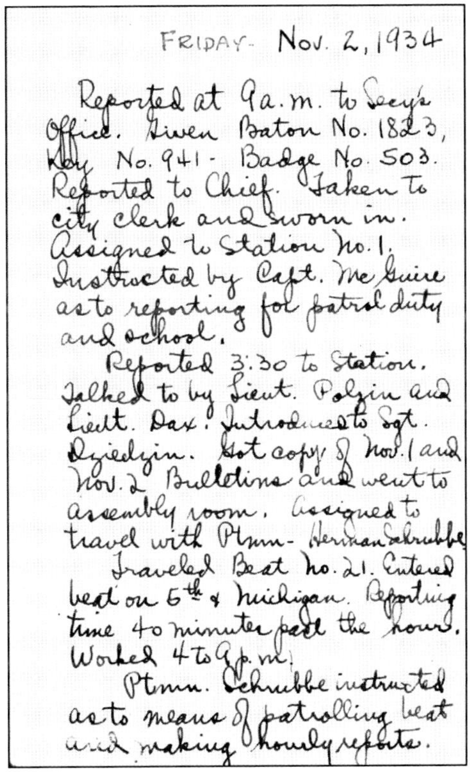

FRIDAY- Nov. 2, 1934

Reported at 9 a.m. to Secy's Office. Given Baton No. 1823, Key No. 941 - Badge No. 503. Reported to Chief. Taken to city clerk and sworn in. Assigned to Station No. 1. Instructed by Capt. McGuire as to reporting for patrol duty and school.

Reported 3:30 to Station. Talked to by Lieut. Polzin and Lieut. Dax. Introduced to Sgt. Dziedzin. Got copy of Nov. 1 and Nov. 2 Bulletins and went to assembly room. Assigned to travel with Ptmn- Herman Schrubbe.

Traveled Beat No. 21. Entered beat on 5th & Michigan. Reporting time 40 minutes past the hour. Worked 4 to 9 p.m.

Ptmn. Schrubbe instructed as to means of patrolling beat and making hourly reports.

PATROLMAN'S DAYBOOK. Eight days before his 25th birthday, George R. Wellauer (1909–1991) reported for duty. His first order was to carefully record all daily activities in a daybook. Shown here are the first two pages of Wellauer's daybook 1, which contains an account of his first day on the job. Rookie patrolmen were routinely given a club and ordered to walk a beat for a shift with a veteran on their first day, and from then on they were on their own. In addition to their daybooks, patrolmen also kept a daily log of arrests. Patrolman Wellauer's daybooks, extant from his first to his last day (November 2, 1934, to February 5, 1962) are the longest running continual series for this early time period. (Author's collection).

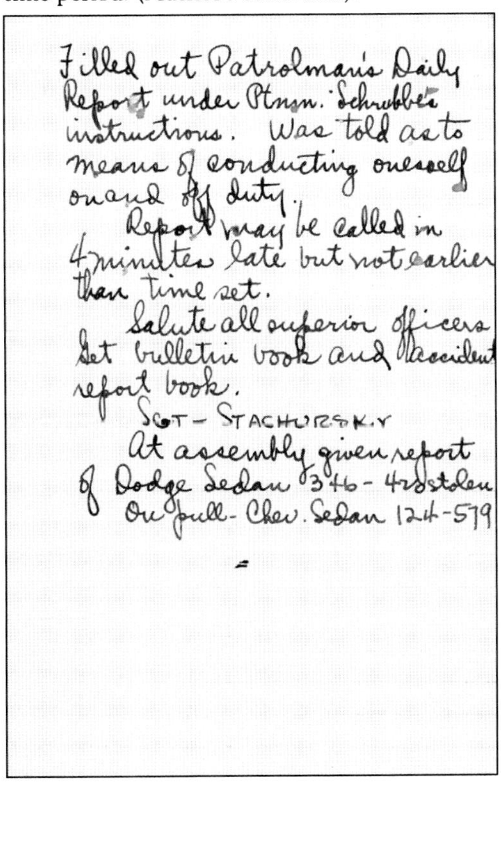

Filled out Patrolman's Daily Report under Ptmn. Schrubbe's instructions. Was told as to means of conducting oneself on and off duty.

Report may be called in 4 minutes late but not earlier than time set.

Salute all superior officers. Get bulletin book and accident report book.

SGT - STACHURSKY

At assembly given report of Dodge Sedan 346-428 stolen. On pull - Chev. Sedan 124-579

The Safety Building and Classroom. The department moved into the newly built Safety Building, leaving behind the old station at Broadway and Wells Streets. The new central administrative headquarters was located at 935 North Eighth Street, as seen here in February 1935. It was also home to the police training school. By the end of the year, the police department employed 1,152 persons. The training school was under the immediate supervision of Capt. Hubert Dax, who succeeded Capt. Floyd McGuire. For the first 30 days, all newly appointed members of the department were required to attend three hours of school each morning for theoretical training and travel with an older member for five hours each evening to receive practical experience. After the 30-day period, all members were required to attend the school once each week. Examinations were given at intervals to rate the efficiency of members. The classroom in the picture below is the larger of the two training rooms located in the Safety Building.

SHOOTING GALLERY. Recruits learned the proper use of service revolvers, rifles, shotguns, and machine guns on this range located in the basement of the police training school in the Safety Building. Regular target practice on a modified practical pistol course was mandatory. Officers had no ear protection at this time, and many, particularly the range masters, suffered impaired hearing as a consequence.

MOUNTED OFFICERS. The Mounted Police Patrol began in 1929. Four patrolmen were assigned to mounted duty, and in 1931, two additional patrolmen and one relief patrolman were added. Six policemen and their steeds were photographed at Milwaukee's lakefront (Juneau Park) in June 1934. The Cudahy Towers dominate the background. From left to right are Lt. Frank Kowaleski on Rex, William Huebner on Buster, Harry Kridler on Jerry, Warren Fidlin on Tommy, George Williams on Buddy, and Joseph Widor on Lucky.

"LADY LUCK" RAN OUT. Confiscated gambling paraphernalia is being incinerated at the Whitefish Bay city dump on Port Washington and Bender Roads under the direction of Deputy Inspector Hugo Goehlen. Illegal gambling in Milwaukee existed in many forms. There was racing, dice, roulette, poker, lottery, slot and pinball machines, and the numbers racket. Police periodically raided gamblers' dens in residential or commercial neighborhoods, or even aboard boats in the harbor.

RADIO TRANSMITTER ROOM. This equipment was located at the Third District (West Side) Station on North Twelfth and West Vine Streets when this photograph was taken in 1932. The police shortwave radio station, WPDK, was later transferred to the new station on Forty-seventh Street and West Vliet Street in 1937, where tests indicated that reception would improve.

CAPTAIN'S AND LIEUTENANT'S OFFICE. These photographs provide a rare look inside the Second District Station in 1935. Note the gun cabinet against the wall and Chief Jacob G. Laubenheimer Jr.'s portrait over the desk.

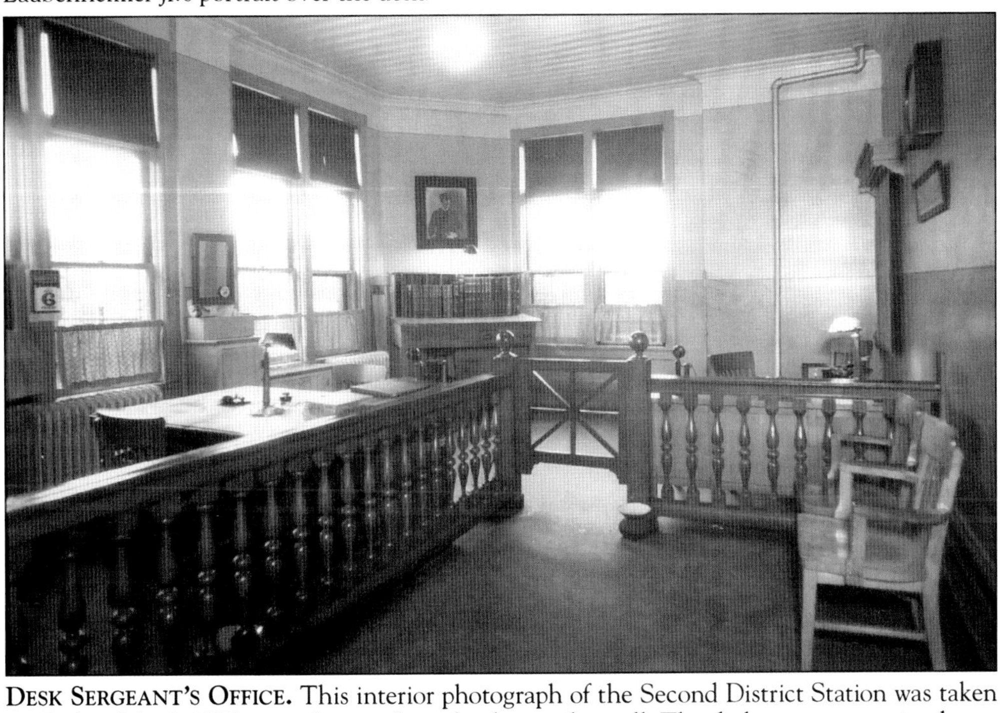

DESK SERGEANT'S OFFICE. This interior photograph of the Second District Station was taken on Friday, July 6, 1935, according to the calendar on the wall. The desk sergeant was in charge of administration. He was also responsible for the feeding and safety of prisoners.

Assembly Room, 1935. A table and a few chairs lightly furnish the assembly room, where officers met each day for roll call, at the Second District Station. Note the photographs of suspects fastened on a wallboard to the left. After Prohibition, policemen could not drink or smoke while in uniform. If they did, the men were subject to fines or could be deprived of days off.

Ladies' Cell Room, 1935. The separate, but most likely equal, accommodations for women prisoners at the Second District Station are shown here.

DESK SERGEANT'S OFFICE. This photograph was taken on Wednesday, July 11, 1935, at the Fourth District Station. Note the pay phone and Chief Jacob G. Laubenheimer Jr.'s portrait hanging on the wall. The board behind the desk reads, "Sign Pay Roll."

PATROLMEN'S ASSEMBLY, 1935. This is the room where the men of the Fourth District Station gathered each day before their shifts. Notice the wanted posters on the bulletin board and the spittoons, strategically placed around the room. The general appearance of the assembly rooms varied little between stations.

Vehicles on Parade. Department photographer Frank Schmidt documented a number of recently purchased vehicles in front of the new Milwaukee County Courthouse in 1936. This new Harley-Davidson motorcycle is equipped with an optional speedometer, particularly helpful in police work. A radio box is mounted on the rear. The rider is wearing leather gauntlets, which were heavy, protective gloves. The new wagon (below) has a sleek new line and running board typical of the 1930s.

AMBULANCE AND SQUAD CAR. The police provided first aid services and conveyance to the Milwaukee County General Hospital in times of need (above). Police squad car No. 2 glistens in the rain outside the new Milwaukee County Courthouse (below).

FUNERAL. Chief Jacob G. Laubenheimer Jr. "died in harness" after serving 15 years as chief. In total, he was with the MPD for 44 years. A lavish funeral was held in the large Milwaukee Auditorium on August 27, 1936, that was followed by a procession on Wisconsin Avenue, attended by thousands.

CHIEF JOSEPH T. KLUCHESKY (1936–1945). Chief Joseph T. Kluchesky rose through the ranks from traffic patrolman, bodyguard to the mayor, and superintendent of the Bureau of Identification, to being the so-called wartime chief. He was known for his Socialist leanings. Kluchesky was born on October 22, 1890, in Wisconsin and died in January 1965. (Courtesy of the Milwaukee Police Department.)

“FORT ON WHEELS.” In 1936, the MPD purchased a massive, bulletproof vehicle, the first armored car of its kind in the nation. This most unusual but formidable vehicle was called “Fort on Wheels.” It was delivered by the manufacturer to the Chicago area by train and then driven to Milwaukee by members of the department. The weight of the vehicle was so great that all four tires gave out before it reached the city limits. It was around for years after, but it did not get much use. This rare interior view, taken in 1941, shows room for seating about 12 officers and reveals Spartan accommodations.

NEW THIRD DISTRICT STATION. Two officers stand outside the new station, which was dedicated on September 2, 1937. Located on the south side of West Vliet and North Forty-seventh Streets (4719 West Vliet Street), it replaced the old Vine Street Station. The boundaries of the first and third precincts were redrawn when the new station opened. The building was designed by Charles E. Malig, City of Milwaukee staff architect, and was constructed at a cost of $140,000. Malig was involved in the design of most of the police and fire stations built in Milwaukee between 1911 and 1949. His designs were primarily examples of the art deco style that was popular from the mid-1920s to the 1940s. His buildings were sturdy, conservative, and utilitarian. Mayor Daniel W. Hoan and other city officials attended the dedication. The building's rear addition was constructed in 1959. At that time, construction workers removed streetcar tracks embedded in Vliet Street that ran past the front of the station. Streetcars were being retired from service throughout the city that year.

Daring and Deadly Luick Dairy Robbery. Detective George Raabe was killed and two uniformed officers were wounded during a gun battle that raged in the main plant of the Luick Dairy Company at 1132 North Sixth Street on November 2, 1937. The officers surprised three bandits who were trying to break into the company safe. At the scene of the crime, police point to bullet holes in the walls. Police felled accomplice Atkins near the safe, visible below. A second bandit was captured and a third robber, designated by police as the suspect who shot Raabe, escaped in a shower of bullets. Two hostages escaped injury by throwing themselves on the floor during the gun battle. Raabe had been appointed to the force on May 27, 1929.

"Straw Boxes." The first call boxes were tall, enclosed kiosks with a police telephone inside that officers used to call headquarters once each hour. They kept rain gear, and sometimes even their prisoners, inside. In frigid weather, a bale of straw was placed on the floor to insulate feet from the cold. The old boxes could still be seen in city yards, such as this one, well into the 1930s.

Flashing Blue Light. Cast-iron call boxes weighing up to 90 pounds were eventually placed on street corners throughout the city. These boxes were equipped with a blue light, usually mounted on top. The purpose of the light was to notify officers on patrol of a waiting message. A flashing light was a signal to all officers who might see it to go immediately to the call box and determine the nature of the alert.

BADGES. This photograph, dated 1938, shows an assortment of coat and hat badges representing the various ranks within the department. From left to right are (first row) captain, lieutenant, sergeant, and patrolman; (second row) captain, detective, and patrolman.

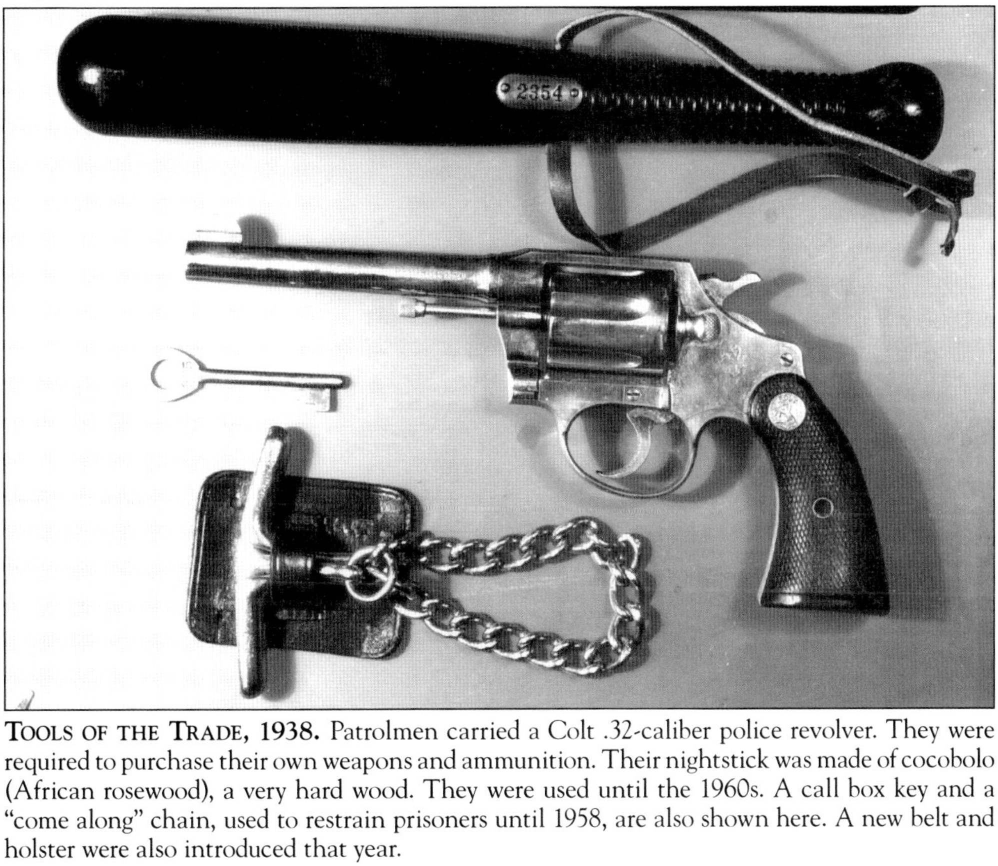

TOOLS OF THE TRADE, 1938. Patrolmen carried a Colt .32-caliber police revolver. They were required to purchase their own weapons and ammunition. Their nightstick was made of cocobolo (African rosewood), a very hard wood. They were used until the 1960s. A call box key and a "come along" chain, used to restrain prisoners until 1958, are also shown here. A new belt and holster were also introduced that year.

POLICEMEN VERSUS FIREMEN. The fierce rivalry between city policemen's and firemen's baseball teams, started at the end of the 19th century, continued annually. Caught on camera in a friendly handshake, Chief Joseph T. Kluchesky (left) and Fire Chief Peter Steinkellner appear cordial just before the big game at Borchert Field on July 9, 1938.

HIGH-TECH ADVERTISING. The department found unique and inexpensive ways to advertise for new recruits during the Depression. This Chrysler sedan, parked in front of a local restaurant, is decked out with recruitment signs, as ordered by the chief in April 1939.

Five

The 1940s

During the 1940s, the MPD enhanced its national reputation for lower burglary rates and fewer major crimes. In 1940, improvements in safety regulations led to Milwaukee's traffic fatality rate being the fourth lowest in the country. The department put strong emphasis on courtesy and respect. These were dangerous times, and the department, like other institutions, shifted its emphasis during the war years.

In addition to their peacetime duties, detectives and patrolmen assumed special wartime duties that were defined as follows: "Special training in and use of knowledge pertaining to sabotage, arson, war gas, and bombs. To acquire a general military knowledge of any and all factors necessary for the well-being of people, civilian police handling, and protection of the civilian population."

An auxiliary police force was formed to assist in the event of an emergency. Its numerous duties were performed under the supervision of a regular policeman. It proved extremely useful and continues to serve today.

Chief Joseph T. Kluchesky designed and built a new bomb-disposal wagon, the first of its kind in the nation, "just in case." He had reason for concern. The previous year, a small bomb exploded in Sears, Roebuck and Company's north side store. Two police stations also had incurred minor damage due to bombings in 1935. When the chief heard about threats of another bombing in a bizarre extortion plot, he wondered what members of his department would do if summoned to remove a live bomb. At the same time, he was aware that saboteurs could target industries in the city involved in war production. So he secretly ordered an old patrol wagon (vintage 1928) converted into a bomb wagon. The vehicle was pressed into service in February 1941 and was kept at the Second District Station on South Sixth and West Mineral Streets.

Following World War II, an extraordinary number of new personnel (1,000), many of them returning veterans, were hired during Chief John W. Polcyn's term. In response, he formed the Personnel Bureau, which proved most helpful. Polcyn activated a narcotics squad and established a special intelligence squad to investigate and curb organized crime.

NATION'S FIRST "BOMB WAGON." It looks like a small coal wagon except for the markings "Explosives, Dangerous." This unique vehicle was intended for the conveyance of bombs to a spot where they could be exploded without endangering lives or property. The back of the driver's cab was replaced by a heavy steel hopper of boiler plate and shaped to direct the blast of an explosion upward through the open top. The hopper was five feet square at the top and three feet square at the bottom. In the photograph below, Capt. Robert Sandow (left) and patrolman Frank Hodach, members of the Bomb Squad, gingerly apply two basic principles of bomb protection, distance and barrier, as they practice removing a suspicious package from the front of a building in 1941. The police ran several tests at a gravel pit outside the city using bombs of all sizes to make sure the vehicle was worthy of claims. The springs on the old chassis were reinforced, and one-and-a-half-inch-thick bulletproof glass was installed to protect the driver.

CONFRONTATION. Labor and management disputes at large local corporations like Allis-Chalmers Manufacturing Company in 1941 often led to brutal clashes with police that resulted in multiple injuries on both sides. Water hoses and tear gas were used to break up disturbances. On April 1, the department's "Fort on Wheels," 22 feet of armor plate manned by sharpshooters, was dispatched to the scene. Offenders were arrested and charged with unlawful assemblage and rioting. This shiny new patrol wagon was also on-site. Several policemen were struck and punched. In court, a judge asked George R. Wellauer, one of the injured officers, if he had been afraid at the time to arrest his assailant. He replied, "I don't know fear in police work," but that it would not have been "prudent." "You don't make an arrest when there are 15,000 enemies around you."

ROGUES' GALLERY. Large books of criminals' photographs were referred to as the Rogues' Gallery in the early days. Images of lawbreakers with names like "Cat-eye Lil" and "Kelly the Choker" were referred to when inquiries or arrests were made. Later so-called mug shots were viewed on wall-mounted displays such as this one in the Safety Building. Some of the oldest photograph books have been preserved by the Milwaukee Police Historical Society.

CHIEF JOHN W. POLCYN (1945–1957). Chief John W. Polcyn, a Wisconsin native, began his career as a patrolman. He trained recruits in discipline and neatness, using his experience as a former Marine Corps sergeant. Polcyn was honored by many civic, fraternal, religious, and military organizations for his efforts to keep Milwaukee crime free with the best police protection possible, including national recognition by FBI director J. Edgar Hoover and U.S. attorney general Ramsey Clark. He died in 1959.

MURAL. This colorful mural, portraying the department's history, was produced in conjunction with the centennial anniversary of the incorporation of the City of Milwaukee in 1846. This photograph was taken at the Cavalcade of Culture in the Milwaukee Auditorium. The mural is currently on permanent display at the Milwaukee Police Safety Academy on Teutonia Avenue. The "Salute to Milwaukee's Finest" float features a squad, children, old and new call boxes, and officers in period uniforms. By 1946, Milwaukee residents thought their city was the safest in America.

PAL. The Police Athletic League (PAL) was established in 1947, sponsored by the Youth Aid Bureau. Its goal was to provide recreation for youth between the ages of 5 and 18. Sporting activities, staffed by volunteer police officers, provided a way for the police department to interact with the community in a non–law enforcement way. Volunteer officers were great role models and mentors. The PAL's baseball teams attracted hundreds of boys. This 1947 photograph shows patrolman George R. Wellauer (back row) and his team, which was sponsored by Ziemer sausage, a local establishment. Once a year, an impressive number of trophies were placed on display. These are the 1948 PAL champions (below). (Above, author's collection.)

WINTER UNIFORMS, 1947. Motorcycle officers pose for the camera in their "Benny" jackets in the Safety Building garage. The jacket, considered quite comfortable and practical by most of the officers, was a heavy winter coat, lined with brown fur. It was made of soft, resilient leather. The name *Benny* comes from *Benjamin*, a slang term for a man's loose-fitting overcoat.

DEWEY IN MILWAUKEE. Thomas E. Dewey, Republican governor of New York and presidential candidate in 1948, and his wife are seen here surrounded by bodyguards and Milwaukee policemen on a visit to Milwaukee.

BOWLING TEAM, 1948. Officers engaged in a variety of team sports in addition to baseball. In the fall and winter months, bowling was a popular pastime.

BASKETBALL TEAM. The MPD basketball team is shown here in March 1949. On the right are coach Frank Brasile, from the Youth Aid Bureau, and Raymond A. Dahl, on the left.

AFRICAN AMERICANS. Four policemen, including Felmers Chaney, stand behind detectives Lonnie Spencer (left) and Calvin Moody (right). The photograph was taken in 1949 at the police academy. Vernice E. Chenault Gallimore, policewoman and the first female African American appointed to the MPD on June 7, 1946, is also shown. She was 27 years old. Dorothy G. Strong, aged 26, was also appointed that day, augmenting the existing policewoman force of two.

"IN THE BARN." The MPD owned three Cadillac ambulances by the end of the decade. They were purchased because of their smooth ride, dependable handling, and reliability. Policemen who drove them report that there were times when citizens refused to be conveyed in the less opulent police squad/ambulances because they gave a rougher ride than the more streamlined Cadillacs.

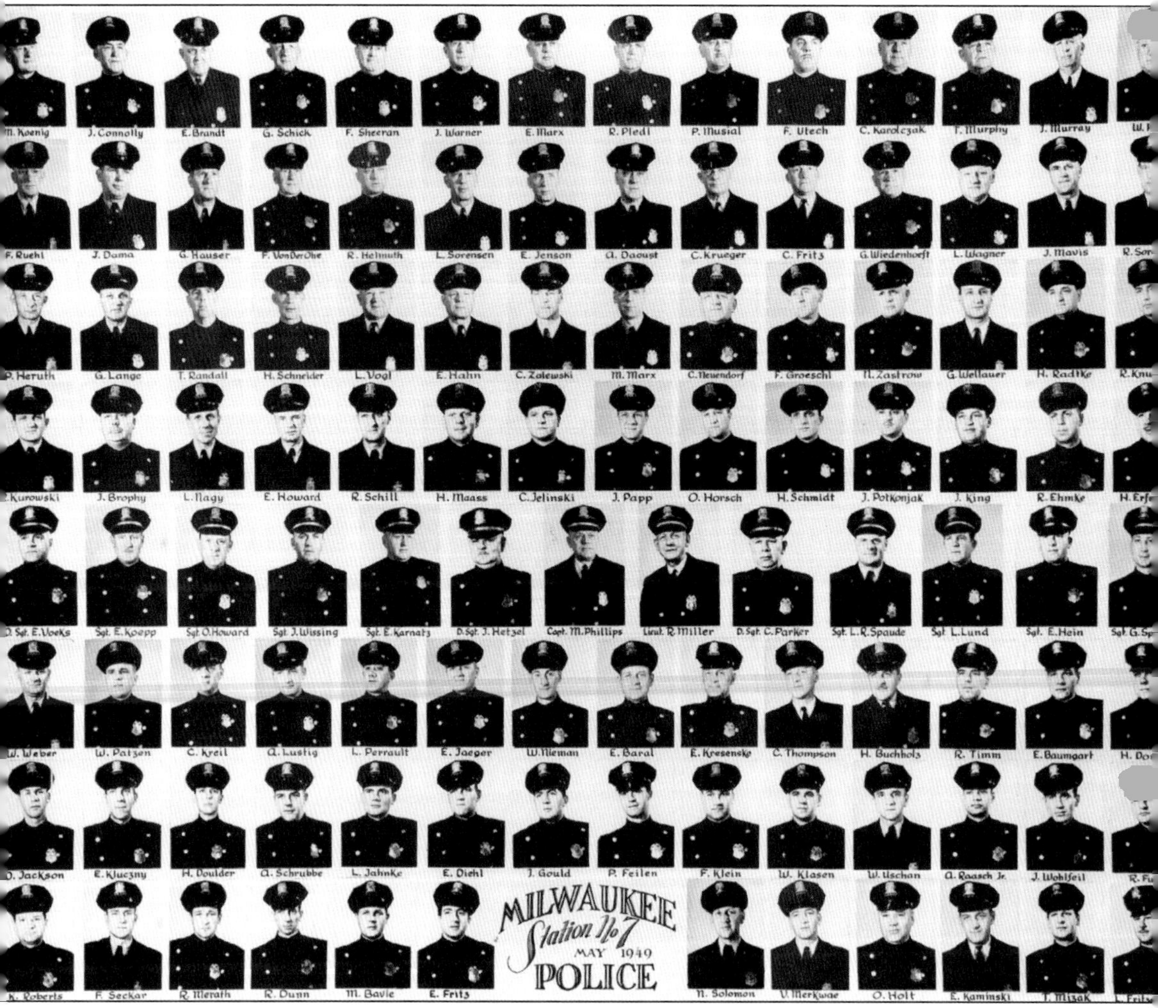

MEN OF SEVEN. This photograph identifies the men assigned to the Seventh District Station, Thirty-sixth Street and West Auer Avenue, in May 1949. Capt. M. Phillips and Lt. R. Miller were in charge. It is only one of two group photographs from this station known to exist. (Author's collection.)

Six

The 1950s

Sandwiched in between the war years and the rebellious and turbulent 1960s, the 1950s were more tranquil times—the "Eisenhower years." Following World War II, the whole country, and the birth rate, was booming. Everything seemed so safe, sane, and secure in Milwaukee. Public relations messages from the MPD assured citizens that "the policeman is your friend." Community-wide programs for bicycle and traffic safety kept police in touch with youth, and Milwaukeeans enjoyed a real sense of peace and well-being.

Coronet magazine presented the MPD with an award on February 20, 1952, commending the city as the "most crime free metropolis in the nation." Three years earlier, the MPD's Detective Bureau was presented with the Call the Police Valor Award, "for Courage, Intelligence, Devotion to Duty as Guardian of the Law."

By mid-decade, the principal function of police communications was to serve and assist the officer on the street, whose prompt, intelligent appraisal of a situation activated all the department facilities to aid him. Communication was both interdepartmental and intradepartmental. Methods included written reports, telephone, telegraph, radio, and "handie-talkie" (the trade name for a portable two-way radio). The Milwaukee Police Telephone System was a city-owned, private network of telephone lines completely independent of the public telephone system (interdepartmental). In the event of a power outage or public utility collapse, the department's system would continue to function through the many call boxes placed throughout the city.

Chief Howard O. Johnson began the practice of recognizing exemplary citizens who assisted the department in some significant manner. He also established Constitution Day in Milwaukee on September 18, 1958, to honor the adoption of the U.S. Constitution. Constitution Day is now observed nationwide. It was his proudest accomplishment.

In 1959, the peace was shattered by the news of the tragic death of Sgt. Raymond Nencki, who was killed while on duty on October 5, 1959. He was posthumously awarded the Medal of Merit by the National Police Officers Association of America "in recognition of outstanding heroism, valor and meritorious service above and beyond the call of duty." He also received the MPD's highest award, the Class A Citation.

MEMORIAL DAY PARADE. Members of the MPD march south on Ninth Street in platoons of about 50 men each. In the September 1976 issue of the *Milwaukee Badge*, retired patrolman George R. Wellauer described the uniform he wore and the experience. The choker-type dress coat "was uncomfortable, hard to keep clean, not adaptable to weather, and certainly not complimentary to the physical appearance of an officer, especially if he had a little weight in the fore-front. The nightstick, flashlight, and pistol made horrible bulges at the rear and sides. No one of course, 'appreciated' the idiocy of that monstrosity called the dress coat until he had to march three miles in the Memorial Day parade wearing that bag, with a celluloid collar threatening to decapitate the wearer and white gloves filling with sweat while the sun glared down and the thermometer boiled at 95 degrees. And there was no compensatory time off or pay for the overtime. Work until 8 a.m., be at the assembly point at 12:30 p.m., start marching at 2 p.m., almost die from heat exhaustion, but be darned sure you didn't miss midnight roll call."

CHIEF POLCYN'S BAND. It is not often that one sees the chief of police with his own polka band. Interestingly, *Polcyn* (pronounced "POLT-sin") is derived from the ancient first name *Pol~ka*, a Pomeranian variant of a name seen elsewhere in Poland as *Pelka*. However, this *Polka* has nothing to do with the dance. The suffix *yn* means "kin or son of," so Polcyn would mean nothing more than the "kin of Pol~ka."

EQUIPMENT DISPLAY. This wall-mounted display of equipment routinely found in combination squad/ambulances includes a backboard, stretcher, shotguns, shells, and bandages.

CADILLAC. This ambulance, photographed on June 21, 1950, was one of the last luxury ambulances that the department owned. They were replaced a few years later by Fords, which were also reliable but cheaper to maintain.

HARLEY-DAVIDSON. This 1949 Hydroglide Harley-Davidson motorcycle was photographed in 1950. It was fitted with a siren and box radio equipment. It also had a hydraulic front fork.

SQUAD NO. 134, 1950. This Ford Coach, with a big red light on the roof, was one of a growing fleet. Two-way radios were installed in police cars for the first time in 1943. Before that, dispatchers could call cars but the officers would have to stop and phone in to the station to respond and get further instructions.

SERVI-CARS. In 1941, the city purchased two three-wheeled motorcycles, or Servi-cars, that were primarily used to enforce parking laws in posted zones. The officer marked tires with chalk and returned later. If the vehicle was still there, a ticket was issued. The Servi-cars had left-hand throttle controls. They proved expensive to maintain and were impractical in inclement weather. They were eventually replaced by "parking checker," or later "parking enforcement," Jeeps.

"PRESENT BATONS." Officers convened at roll call every day before their shifts began. First the officers saluted a superior officer with their batons, and then they removed their service revolvers from their holsters and emptied the bullets in their hands for inspection. The daily bulletin was read and distributed, and the line of officers was inspected for a clean and neat appearance. This usually took 10 to 15 minutes. The squad men went to their vehicles and the beat men followed the sergeant (in a single-file line behind him) to the street.

TRAFFIC BUREAU, 1952. This newly remodeled Traffic Bureau counter in the downtown Milwaukee Safety Building (room 208) was very busy every day.

NEW SECOND DISTRICT STATION. This station opened on Thursday, August 20, 1953, at 3:00 p.m. It was located at 245 West Lincoln Avenue. The building cost $400,000 and was the first new station built since 1937. The second police district (1003 South Sixth Street) and fourth police district (2156 South Allis Street) were combined to form the new second district.

TELEPHONE SWITCHBOARD. This photograph shows the telephone switchboard at Milwaukee Police Headquarters on September 28, 1954. Chief operator Joseph Schraufnagel is seated at his desk. Other operators in this picture are Fred Caffrey, Harold Reinelt, Leo Kopecki, Joseph Potkonjak, and George Maederer. When the handle inside a call box was pulled, the machines in the background would register the origin of the call. Help was dispatched to the proper location immediately.

AMBULANCE AND SQUADS. When the department added to its fleet, the vehicles were usually photographed before license plates were installed, as was the case with this ambulance. The inside of the vehicle is on display to show off its state-of-the-art equipment. In 1954, the MPD conveyed a total of 17,105 persons in 13,521 ambulance runs. In preparation for ambulance duty, officers were told that the large number of conveyances also increased the chances that they might have to assist in or actually deliver a baby in a police ambulance or in a private home. The Ford squad cars were sturdy and reliable and a popular choice of police departments in the 1950s. These are "needle cars" (below). Officers used them to monitor speeders.

TOP SHOOTERS. Members of the 1956 Milwaukee police team No. 1 winners, police officer Sharafinski, police officer Quin O'Brien, police officer Budney, and police officer Psarros, proudly display their award, Milwaukee County Center Fire Pistol League Elimination Tournament. The Milwaukee team captured the title again in 1959–1960, with two new members, police officer Ken Koltermann and Sgt. Wilbert "Bullets" Neiman. O'Brien was later killed in a shootout at the courthouse in Waukesha County.

CHIEF HOWARD O. JOHNSON (1957–1964). Howard O. Johnson was appointed patrolman on May 7, 1934, and after seven years was promoted to patrol sergeant in 1941. Exactly eight years after, he was promoted to lieutenant. In the winter of 1952, Johnson was appointed captain, and on January 22, 1954, he advanced to deputy inspector, a position he held until he was appointed chief. Johnson allowed short-sleeved shirts when a survey indicated that 93 percent of the men preferred them. (Courtesy of the Milwaukee Police Department.)

NO "FIX" HERE. A motorcycle officer issues a citation along a boulevard on a summer day. Paul de Kruif, a writer for *Ladies' Home Journal*, cited an absence of what he called a common curse in most cities, the "fix." He wrote, "When you get a traffic ticket in Milwaukee, you pay a fine. You don't find a friend on the police force who tears it up and says, 'forget it.'"

COCKPIT. An inside view of a police motorcycle shows a Motorola radio speaker, a speedometer, and a personal good luck piece or talisman with a good old Milwaukee connection—a Schlitz beer tap pull—on the gas tank.

METRO. This is a 1958 International Harvester (IH) van. The Internationals were a favorite with police departments because of their durability.

SAFETY FIRST. Police officers made frequent stops at neighborhood schools and playgrounds to inspect bicycles, check registrations, and offer safety tips to youngsters throughout the 1950s. Many Milwaukee schoolchildren made their first trip to a police station to buy a license for their bicycles. The inspection, shown here in June 1959, was intended to insure a safe summer holiday for the students.

ROYAL VISIT. Chief Howard O. Johnson (center) greets King Peter II of Yugoslavia (left) during his visit to Wisconsin. Forced to leave his country in 1941, King Peter II, who was deposed by the Yugoslavian Communist Constituent Assembly in 1945, eventually settled in the United States.

FIFTH DISTRICT STATION. The ground was broken for a new station in 1958 at Fourth and Locust Streets (2920 North Fourth Street). The original Fifth District Station, located at Third and Hadley Streets, was demolished shortly thereafter. The first roll call was held in the new facility on September 1, 1960. The first station head was Capt. William Huebner. The building, completely remodeled in 1994, was reopened in 1995.

Seven

THE 1960s

The 1960s came in like a lamb and went out like a lion. At the outset, crime was relatively low and citizens, for the most part, obeyed the law and respected the police. Society changed and so did police work—at a lightning pace. Officers received accelerated training to deal with the rampant misuse of drugs and other controlled substances. They had to learn how to protect themselves and citizens against social unrest in the streets while helping with labor disputes and dealing with increasingly more vicious crimes and perpetrators.

By 1960, the MPD had acquired the most modern methods of communication. The MPD had three switchboards, one located in the Safety Building, one in the Second District Station, and one in the Fifth District Station. The head switchboard in the Safety Building had five stations for operators to work. Twenty-seven circuits or lines were connected to this board, each of which was connected to an average of 18 separate call boxes.

In March 1964, Milwaukee's first Hispanic officer, Procopio "Nick" Sandoval Jr., a former U.S. Army policeman of Mexican (Spanish) heritage, joined the force.

Milwaukee had a tough chief in difficult times. Chief Harold A. Breier's 20-year tenure was marked by turbulent times and controversy, to which he seldom yielded. His most severe test perhaps came during the civil disturbances (riots) of 1967 and the fair-housing protests. Forty-four years of his life were devoted to service in law enforcement. After he passed away in 1998, the Hon. Gerald D. Kleczka, representative from Wisconsin, memorialized him in the *Congressional Record*, proclaiming, "Mr. Breier's name was synonymous with law and order in Milwaukee."

Open housing marches in 1967 were staged to obtain equitable treatment for all citizens. After several properties were torn down on the near north side the year before, the housing crunch touched many black families. Activists picketed Milwaukee aldermen's homes and marched from the north side to the south side protesting discrimination. When they met with hostile crowds, police used tear gas to disperse them. A fair-housing ordinance was finally passed in April 1968.

Milwaukee went through many changes and transformations in the 1960s. Its population declined, and people were moving to the suburbs. The MPD was having difficulty finding new recruits and stepped up its efforts to find good men.

CHRISTMAS PARTY. The annual Christmas party, held in the Safety Building gymnasium, was a highlight for hundreds of policemen's children. A clown and singer on center stage played to a full house on December 17, 1960. The event featured music, acrobatics, a chimpanzee act, treats, and, of course, an appearance by Santa himself. Balloons proudly proclaiming "My Daddy is a Policeman" were real crowd-pleasers. There were 1,848 members of the department in December 1960.

EMERGENCY RESPONSE. Inspector Raymond A. Dahl (left) and Capt. Charles Kuhn survey a display of equipment from the newly purchased Squad 310 in 1960. Squad 310, as it was called, was sent to extreme emergency situations. It was parked at the Fifth District Station.

BUSTED. Narcotic officers display a large quantity of marijuana, stashed in tobacco and coffee cans and fruit jars, seized in a drug raid. Ralph Brown, who later became captain in the Detective Bureau, is on the right. Marijuana was a known street drug for decades, but its use became more widespread in the 1960s, particularly with the counterculture that thrived on the city's east side and among college students.

DARING RESCUE. This emotional and touching image of an officer tending to an injured boy was captured by *Milwaukee Sentinel* photographer Sherman Gessert on June 17, 1961. He was truly a friend in deed. (Courtesy Journal Sentinel, Inc., reproduced with permission.)

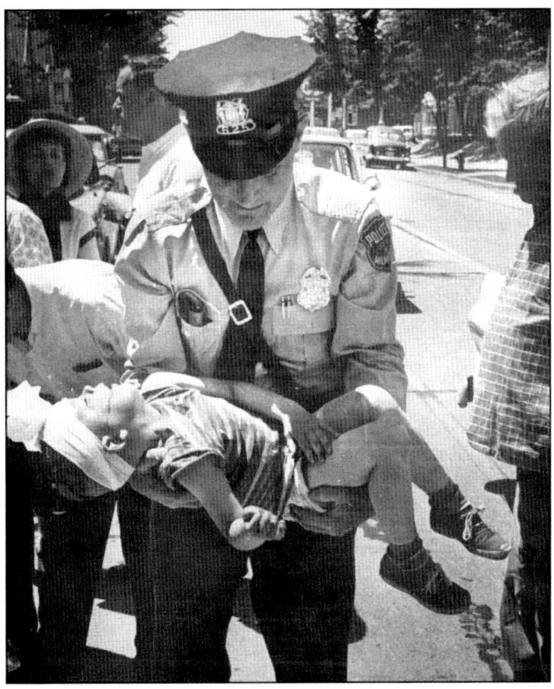

MPD CLERICAL DEPARTMENT, 1962. These are the people working behind the scenes in the Safety Building. They handled the paperwork and helped the department run smoothly. This photograph was taken by E. Kasprzak of the Bureau of Identification.

FINGERPRINTING. Fingerprint identification was first utilized in 1907; however, it was not considered an exact science even as late as the 1930s. In 1940, the police initiated voluntary fingerprinting of school students. Detectives usually took fingerprints at crime scenes and sent them back to the Bureau of Identification where the technical staff did the necessary matching. This display shows the standard apparatus used in 1963.

POLICE BOAT, 1964. This vessel joins with the *Harbor Seagull* in a search for evidence. The first police boat, *Killjoy I* (launched July 1922), was equipped with a spotlight and horn and traveled up to 15 knots per hour. Police were on the alert for vandalism, thievery, and "night romancing" along the river and lake. The river police station was located at the west end of the North Avenue viaduct. Today police jurisdiction extends 48 miles east of the coast.

"NEEDLE CAR." The name for a speed watch car was "needle car," so called because of a needle pointer on a machine mounted on the console that moved to indicate the speed in miles per hour. Special rubber-coated wires were stretched across the road and connected to a machine that measured the speed of vehicles as they passed over it. This squad was photographed on April 7, 1964. (Courtesy of the Milwaukee Police Department.)

"**Bread Wagon.**" Patrol wagons, previously all black since the early days, were replaced by white vans in the 1960s. The vehicle was nicknamed "bread wagon" and "pie wagon" because of the resemblance to the delivery trucks used by the Wonder Bread and Jaeger Baking Companies that were located in Milwaukee.

Combo, 1964. This is an International combination squad/ambulance made locally by IH. (Courtesy of the Milwaukee Police Department.)

POLICE PICNIC. Off-duty policemen and their families enjoy a warm day in June at the annual police picnic held at Jackson Park on Milwaukee's south side. In earlier times, picnics also convened at Mitchell and Washington Parks. For a quick lunch, this officer warms a can of pork and beans and a can of Milwaukee's own Frank's Sauerkraut on the barbecue grill while his youngster casts a watchful eye.

STAYING COOL. "Milwaukee's finest" serve up cool glasses of a popular local product, Schlitz, "the Beer That Made Milwaukee Famous." The day's events included scheduled activities for the children and softball competitions for the men.

CHIEF HAROLD A. BREIER (1964–1984). A product of Milwaukee's south side, Harold A. Breier worked in a number of blue-collar jobs, was a temporary deputy sheriff, and played tackle on an amateur football team called the West Allis Majors before joining the force in 1940. He became a detective on the Vice Squad in 1946. He was promoted to lieutenant in 1954, captain in 1958, deputy inspector in 1960, and inspector of detectives in 1962 and was sworn in as chief of police in 1964. (Courtesy of the Milwaukee Police Department).

NEW FOURTH DISTRICT STATION. The new Fourth District Station opened at 12:01 a.m. on January 1, 1965. It is located at 6929 West Silver Spring Drive.

VETERAN. Master Sgt. Michael Bavle was a Milwaukee police officer and a member of the 5063rd United States Army Garrison (military police) of Milwaukee. He is shown here giving an orientation lecture on the .45-caliber automatic pistol while on active duty at Camp McCoy (August 23, 1965). Several members of the MPD served in the military during the Vietnam era and previous conflicts. Many veterans are members today of the Wisconsin American Legion Milwaukee Police Post 415.

ZOO PATROL. An officer seems to be enjoying his drive past the bears at the Milwaukee County Zoo in April 1966. This Harley-Davidson-manufactured golf cart was specially modified for police use. The carts were also used to patrol Milwaukee parks and parades. They were last used to distribute soft drinks to officers along the route of the Great Circus Parade. The zoo was relocated to Bluemound Road from Washington Park in 1963.

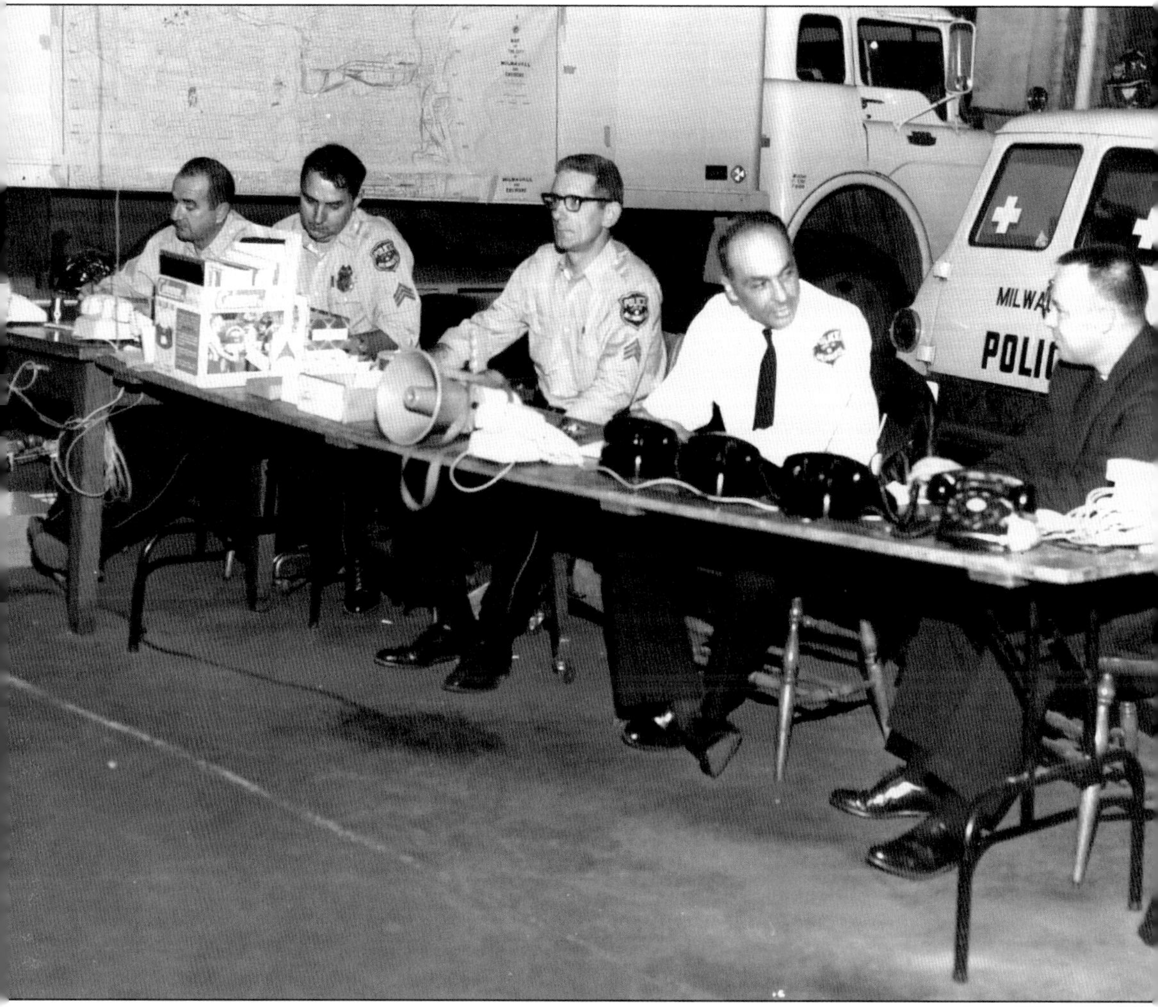

Riots of 1967. The unrest in Milwaukee on July 30 followed similar disturbances in Newark and Detroit. It began in the evening on the near north side in the vicinity of North Third Street when stones, bottles, and bricks were hurled viciously. The sounds of gunfire from hidden snipers and police shooting out streetlights crackled throughout the night. The situation became more serious as property damage and injuries mounted. The MPD reacted swiftly and decisively. An emergency command post was set up in the garage of Schuster's department store. Only three of the men in this photograph are identified: Fred Stein, Robert Blair, and Andrew Busalacchi. Together they were responsible for implementing major decisions during the initial, critical days. Officers grabbed a bit of sleep wherever they could. Men slept in cars and on the top of them, wrapped in heavy blankets. Squad windows were taped to reduce damage from flying rocks and other debris.

TANKS IN THE STREETS. The following day, Mayor Henry Maier and Chief Harold A. Breier called on the National Guard to help control the situation. During this explosive time, over 1,700 arrests were made. Local newspapers ran the headlines "Riots Erupt Again; Sniping, Fires Rage" (August 2), "Area of Riot Tense; Sniper Fire Goes On," and "City Under Curfew for 7 Nights." Streets were virtually empty, except for police and military vehicles.

ALERT. Officers worked 12-hour shifts during the crisis. It was not unusual to see policemen on high alert with shotguns ready. In August, Chief Harold A. Breier created Milwaukee's Tactical Enforcement Unit, which was specially trained to respond to high-risk calls, particularly hostage situations. As a result of the riots, there were three deaths, including one police officer, Bryan Moschea, Ann Mosley, an elderly invalid woman he was protecting, and a young man. Almost 100 serious injuries were reported.

Open Housing Marches. Fr. James Groppi, a Roman Catholic priest, led marchers across the Sixteenth Street viaduct from the north side to Kosciuszko Park on the all-white south side protesting discrimination in August 1967. Groppi and 58 others were arrested for civil disobedience after an assembly at their burned-out headquarters, called the Freedom House. (Courtesy of the Wisconsin Historical Society, Image ID 26541.)

Drive Up and Pay. The department opened a drive-up window on the east side of the Safety Building in February 1968, making it more convenient for citizens to pay traffic tickets and to obtain overnight parking permits. The officer is Valentin Merkwae. After retirement, he was employed as a security guard at Capitol Court, a shopping center on Milwaukee's northwest side. He was fatally wounded on May 7, 1975, by a man he had chased into a store.

Eight

THE 1970s

Violent labor strikes at American Motors, Allen-Bradley, and Schlitz, as well as other civil disturbances in the early 1970s, kept police busy. Members of the MPD staged their own work slowdown, the so-called blue flu, for seven days in January 1971. During this decade, emphasis was placed on improved relations within the community. It was also a period of diversification of the department, improvements in radio and communications systems, and computerization. New badge identifications and a Miricode machine were introduced in 1971. Bulletproof vests were not yet standard equipment. On a lighter note, policemen were allowed to go without ties for the first time in 1972. Squad jackets and caps were redesigned in 1976.

The police training school was relocated from the Safety Building to its current home in the former Madonna High School at 6680 North Teutonia Avenue. The City of Milwaukee purchased the site in August 1972, and the police academy moved in the next day. The facility, only eight years old, was perfectly adapted for use by the department. The school was divided into five basic areas: classrooms, physical training, firearms training, mock crime scenes, and study areas. There is a library on the second floor of the building. Specialized training facilities include a model barroom, called Copper's Corner, because so many crimes take place in taverns, and an apartment complex, with furniture, kitchen appliances, and other amenities. The building is shared with the Milwaukee Fire Department's Bureau of Instruction and Training.

The first woman, Hedwig S. Jessen, retired from the MPD in 1977, after a 25-year career. She rose from clerk to policewoman in 1951, when she was one of seven women in the department to hold that title. While police officers could work anywhere internally, policewomen worked only in the Vice Squad and Youth Aid Bureau.

When the decade ended, the Milwaukee Fire Department took over paramedic duties, and police ambulances were phased out. This ended a long police tradition of first aid and emergency care. The number of deaths that occurred in the line of duty were greater in the 1970s than in any previous decade in MPD history. Eight policemen were shot and killed, and four others died in accidents.

BICYCLE AUCTION. Each year, the department auctioned off its vast inventory of unclaimed bicycles and other goods to the public. Many girls and boys in the city owned at least one bike purchased from an MPD sale. This sale took place in June 1970. Trinity Evangelical Lutheran Church on Ninth Street and Highland Boulevard is visible in the background.

ADAM-12 MEETS THE MPD. Television cops Martin Milner and Kent McCord, stars of the hit series *Adam-12*, stand in formation with Milwaukee policemen. Milner played officer James A. Reed, and McCord was officer Pete Malloy. *Adam-12*, which aired between 1968 and 1975, was created by Jack Webb, who formerly starred in the popular 1950s police show *Dragnet*. Patrolman Nicholas (Nick) Monreal is on the far right.

RECRUITING. The MPD participated at the Wisconsin State Fair in West Allis, a suburb of Milwaukee. Officer Howard Sobczyk (left) and Sgt. Joe Kalivoda are manning a recruiting booth.

MILWAUKEE POLICE SAFETY ACADEMY. All Milwaukee police officers receive extensive training at 6680 North Teutonia Avenue. The academy's goal is to provide a continuing educational and training process that yields a professional police officer and a department that inspires the confidence, respect, and trust of the community they serve. *On Watch*, by sculptor David M. Wanner, stands at the entrance to the academy. It was "dedicated to the guardians of public safety in the City of Milwaukee" in 1990. (Courtesy of Diane Lardinois.)

First Female "Patrolman." Twenty-four-year-old Ada Wright became Milwaukee's first female street "patrolman" in April 1975. She wore the regulation uniform her first day on the job. After Wright's appointment, a federal court ordered the Fire and Police Commission to hire 10 more woman officers. On August 27, 1978, a *Milwaukee Journal* feature, "The Making of a Cop," reported that only 45 of the officers in the police department were female. (Courtesy of Ada Wright.)

Community Relations Mobile Unit. This well-equipped mobile transport, sponsored by the City of Milwaukee and the Fire and Police Commission, carried the department's recruitment and crime prevention messages throughout the city. Citizens were guided through displays titled "Police Services" and "A Citizen's Duty Is to Prevent Crime." The mobile unit was photographed in front of John Muir Junior High School on Seventy-second Street and Silver Spring Drive in 1973.

ARBOR DAY. This ceremony was held on Thursday, April 26, 1973, at the Sixth District Station on West Burnham Street. Pictured from left to right are George R. Wellauer, Chief Harold A. Breier, J. Newcombe, and Capt. Fred Krema. Members of the Retired Police Association planted a tree each Arbor Day to symbolize the service and sacrifice that characterizes police service. These trees honored past and present members of the department in prominent locations. The association hoped that these living memorials would be an enduring testimony to the association's permanence, faith, and usefulness. (Author's collection.)

HARBOR PATROL. The MPD extended its reach beyond land by establishing the Underwater Investigation Unit. It was on call day or night for rescues. The Harbor Patrol was established during Chief Howard O. Johnson's term to help stranded boaters, adjunct to the U.S. Coast Guard Harbor Security. This display, manned by Ralph Brunhart, who is seated on the right, was at the Milwaukee Expo Center Boat Show in January 1974.

BOMB SQUAD. Members of the Bomb Squad display the latest equipment in July 1975. They are, from left to right, Edward Sharon, Walter Puhlman, Emil Markovic, John Schroder, Eugene Brown, and George Timm (standing). The explosives wagon in this picture is much improved over the earlier model built in the 1940s. (Courtesy of the Milwaukee Police Department).

SWAT. The MPD's SWAT team was deployed to this Milwaukee residence in July 1978. A combination of teamwork, speed, noise, and stealth are employed when entering a house. Deadly force was available but used only as a last resort in the MPD. (Courtesy of the Historic Photographic Collection/Milwaukee Public Library.)

Nine

From 1980 to the Present

In his State of the Union address, Pres. Jimmy Carter defined the beginning of the decade. "The 1980s have been born in turmoil, strife, and change. This is a time of challenge to our interests and our values and it's a time that tests our wisdom and our skills." The MPD reacted to the challenges of a new age by retooling to meet the new and ever-changing needs of a large urban city. It became adept at not simply responding when called upon but also by offering constructive preventative and problem-solving strategies. At this time, police focused their resources on reducing crime and enhancing the quality of life in the city. The Crime Prevention Unit was founded in 1985. More than ever before, the MPD became even more reflective of the community it served at all levels.

After Chief Harold A. Breier left office in 1984, the term limit was cut to seven years. All chiefs appointed thereafter have served less.

Members of the department were seen at more public events in the 1990s than ever before. The Metropolitan Division policed over 200 major special events each year. The motorcycle and bicycle units were frequently seen patrolling at Summerfest and at the ethnic festivals such as Germanfest and Irishfest, as well as parades. The Historic Mounted Horse Patrol, disbanded in 1948, was revived and was a popular attraction at the Great Circus Parade every July.

The MPD was on hand to provide Pres. Bill Clinton and Chancellor Helmut Kohl with a safe and successful experience when they met in Milwaukee for their so-called Sausage Summit on May 27, 1996.

In December 2002, Milwaukee's Lt. Andrew Anewenter was recognized as the longest-serving officer in the nation's history. The National Law Enforcement Officers Memorial Fund (NLEOMF) chose him as its Officer of the Month. At the time, Anewenter was assigned to the Property Crimes Division of the MPD.

Currently the MPD is a thoroughly modern and efficient organization, consisting of three major bureaus: the Administration Bureau, the Patrol Bureau, and the Criminal Investigation Bureau. The department continues to faithfully serve the community, strengthened in its steadfast commitment by the same noble ideals and strong code of ethics that have characterized the force for 152 years.

NEW DESIGN. The interior of this newly redesigned squad car was unveiled to the public in September 1980. Squads were not air-conditioned until later because the chief thought if officers cruised in a squad with open windows and at low speed, it would be easier to hear outside noises and identify trouble. (Courtesy of the Historic Photographic Collection/Milwaukee Public Library.)

SEVENTH DISTRICT STATION. The groundbreaking ceremony for this new station, which was located across the street from the old site on Thirty-sixth Street and Auer Avenue, was attended by dignitaries, including Mayor Henry Maier, in May 1980. The Seventh District Station, shown here, was opened in 1981. (Courtesy of Zimmerman Architectural Studios, Inc.)

PARADE. The Great Circus Parade was a major summer event in downtown Milwaukee. Ornate wagons from the Circus World Museum in Baraboo were brought in by rail. Actor Ernest Borgnine was grand marshal for over 15 years. His wife, Tova, was a ringmaster. Ernest called the parade "clean, wholesome, family entertainment." In this photograph, from left to right are Ernest, police officer Leonard Eversdyk, police officer Bagurdes, Tova, and Capt. William E. Gielow. (Courtesy of William E. Gielow.)

CHIEF ROBERT J. ZIARNIK (1984–1989). Robert J. Ziarnik began his career as a patrolman in 1950. Prior to that, he served in the U.S. Navy for three years, the U.S. Army, and the U.S. Coast Guard Reserve. During his career, he was a lieutenant at the First and Fifth Districts, captain in the Vice Squad and the Personnel Bureau, and headed the police academy. He retired from the position of inspector of police in 1983 and came out of retirement in 1984 to serve as chief of police. His service to the department spanned more than 35 years when he retired for a second time as chief in 1989. (Courtesy of William E. Gielow.)

CHIEF PHILIP ARREOLA (1989–1996). Philip Arreola was the first chief of Hispanic heritage. Arreola served on the Detroit Police Department for 27 years, attaining the rank of commander. He also served as chief of the Port Huron (Michigan) Police Department before being named chief in Milwaukee. Arreola, an attorney, received his Juris Doctor degree from Wayne State University in 1985. He is also a 1977 graduate of the FBI's National Academy in Quantico, Virginia. (Courtesy of William E. Gielow.)

WORKING TOGETHER. This photograph, taken in a local park, was featured on the cover of one of the department's annual reports. It represented the theme of "police department and community working together." At the time, the department adopted a philosophy of community-oriented policing. (Courtesy of William E. Gielow.)

CHIEF ARTHUR L. JONES (1996–2003). Chief Arthur L. Jones began his career as a police officer in October 1967. Prior to his appointment as chief, he served as the deputy inspector of police in charge of the Special Operations Bureau. Jones also served in several other capacities, including lieutenant of detectives assigned to the Special Assignment Division, primarily responsible for protecting the mayor. After retirement, he made an unsuccessful bid for mayor. (Courtesy of the Milwaukee Police Department.)

TALKING SQUAD CAR. The first of its kind in the country, the MPD's "talking squad car" and McGruff the Crime Dog deliver crime prevention tips to thousands every year. They often appear at popular events such as the National Night Out, when Milwaukee residents join in community crime prevention efforts by attending block parties, cookouts, and anticrime rallies, or just flicking on their porch lights for the evening in solidarity.

NEWEST STATION. A new state-of-the-art Third District Station and Communications Operations Center, established to serve Milwaukee's west side, was erected in the historic Uptown Crossing area and opened in 2001. One year earlier, civilians replaced police officers as dispatchers in the MPD Communications Division. (Photograph copyright Greg Gent Studios, reproduced with permission; courtesy of Zimmerman Architectural Studios, Inc.)

PATCHES. Over the years, hundreds of Milwaukee police officers have proudly worn the patches on display here.

FALLEN BUT NOT FORGOTTEN. This moving and solemn poster was designed by the MPD's graphic designer, Diane Lardinois, for the ceremony at the Law Enforcement Memorial on MacArthur Square, Milwaukee, in 2000. Photographs of Milwaukee police officers killed in the line of duty frame the bugler. (Courtesy of Diane Lardinois.)

In Memory of Sixty-one Officers who Died in the Line of Duty in Faithful Service to the Citizens of the City of Milwaukee

"Greater love hath no man than this, that he lay down his life for his friends"

Frank Piszczek – 22 Jun 1884
John Kossow – 30 Sep 1899
Ernest Johnson – 15 Sep 1904
Otto H. Flieth – 17 Dec 1908
Peter Gauer – 3 Jul 1909
Frank M. Caswin – 24 Nov 1917
Henry J. Deckert – 24 Nov 1917
Frederick W. Kaiser – 24 Nov 1917
David G. O'Brien – 24 Nov 1917
Charles Seehawer – 24 Nov 1917
Edward Spindler – 24 Nov 1917
Stephen H. Stecker – 24 Nov 1917
Albert Templin – 24 Nov 1917
Paul J. Weiler – 24 Nov 1917
William F. Kaemmerling – 26 Jan 1922
Joseph Kubacki – 24 May 1924
Walter Luedtke – 18 Dec 1924
Harold W. Schmidt – 4 Apr 1925
Hilbert Thurow – 22 Aug 1930
Robert Bahlke – 23 Feb 1932
Richard R. Zingler – 8 Feb 1933
Harry Pieske – 27 Jun 1935
Charles George – 8 Jun 1936
Nels Goodman – 10 Aug 1937
George Raabe – 2 Nov 1937
Joseph Lecher – 21 Mar 1943
Arnold Werner – 10 Jul 1943
Frank Chybowski – 12 Jul 1946
Valentin Adam – 6 Mar 1948
Elmer W. Bates – 23 Aug 1948
Vernon White – 10 Nov 1951
Raymond A. Nencki – 5 Oct 1959
Robert Kraemer – 7 Feb 1963
James J. Rivers – 21 Mar 1966
Ronald T. Hogan – 2 May 1967
Bryan Moschea – 31 Jul 1967
George Fish – 23 Sep 1970
Alan Sroczynski – 8 Nov 1970
Paul DuPlanty – 9 Nov 1971
Gerald Hempe – 31 Jan 1973
Charles T. Smith – 31 Jan 1973
Ronald Reagan – 13 Dec 1973
Thomas G. Matulis – 10 Jul 1974
Robert D. Riley – 10 Jul 1974
Michael Draeger – 28 Dec 1974
Dennis L. Obradovich – 18 Aug 1975
Albert Kohn – 29 Oct 1975
Thomas Kiefer – 25 Nov 1977
John Machajewski – 23 Dec 1981
Charles S. Mehlberg – 23 Dec 1981
Sydney C. Snow – 30 Jan 1982
Rosario J. Collura – 19 Mar 1985
Leonard R. Lesnieski – 19 Mar 1985
Dennis J. Gorlewski – 25 Feb 1987
Roger A. Sterling – 11 May 1987
Steven J. Hasenstab – 19 Aug 1989
Richard E. Wagner – 25 Oct 1990
Michael R. Tourmo – 18 Nov 1990
William A. Robertson – 7 Sep 1994
Michael A. Niehoff – 30 Nov 1994
Wendolyn Tanner – 7 Sep 1996

Rest in Peace For a Job Well Done

ROLL OF HONOR. The MPD and the citizens of Milwaukee mourn the loss of sixty-one fine officers who sacrificed their lives since 1884.

LONGEVITY. Lt. Andrew Anewenter was the longest-serving officer in the nation. He walked the beat, patrolled the city, and investigated crimes, including murders, assaults, thefts, counterfeiting operations, drug trafficking, and a plane crash. He provided security for dignitaries and celebrities, the most notable being Elvis Presley. One of the best-known interdepartmental photographs is that of Anewenter in his now famous fedora that he wore from the time he joined the force in 1942 until his death in 2003, a few weeks after he retired.

NANNETTE H. HEGERTY, 2003–2007. In 1994, Pres. Bill Clinton appointed the MPD's Capt. Nannette Hegerty U.S. marshal for the Eastern District of Wisconsin. She returned to the department in late 2002 to head the sensitive crimes division, and one year later, she became the city's 16th chief of police. (Courtesy of Chief Nannette H. Hegerty.)

AFTERWORD

I joined the ranks of the Milwaukee Police Department in 1976 when there were fewer than 10 female officers. I had to prove myself, but I believe my education, life experience, faith, and true desire to serve others was recognized. In time, I gained experience and was promoted, becoming the first female lieutenant, the first female captain, and eventually the city's first female chief. None of this occurred without hard work, dedication, and the will to succeed.

As chief, I developed a strategic plan, believing all chief executive officers must have a vision and then must develop steps to achieve it. My goal was to reduce crime, especially violent crime. I placed an emphasis on professionalism, and I also wanted to focus on rebuilding trust with the community. I stressed the importance of courtesy, dignity, and respect and encouraged cooperation with other law enforcement agencies and criminal justice entities.

Throughout my 31 years in law enforcement, I have witnessed many changes. As chief for four years, I was able to institute some of those changes. I believe change is good, and the secret to success is remaining flexible. I believe the road to being successful includes openness to new ideas and the courage to forge new ideas.

The Milwaukee Police Department has a long tradition of excellence in policing. I hope that I have enhanced that reputation and have placed the organization in a position to continue quality service and protection to the community for years to come. The men and women of the Milwaukee Police Department work hard each and every day. They are the true heroes who place their lives in danger while performing the difficult tasks associated with public safety. They are the ones who deserve the credit, and they are the ones who will move the Milwaukee Police Department forward.

—Police Chief Nannette H. Hegerty

BIBLIOGRAPHY

Bruce, William George. *History of Milwaukee City and County*. Chicago: S. J. Clarke Publishing Company, 1922.

Creutz, Al, comp. *Glimpses of Milwaukee: Its Fires, Fire and Police Departments*. Milwaukee: self-published, 1893.

Flower, Frank A. *History of Milwaukee, Wisconsin*. Chicago: Western Historical Company, 1881.

"An Illustrated Description of Milwaukee." *Milwaukee Sentinel*, March 1890.

"The Making of a Cop." *Milwaukee Journal Insight*, August 27, 1978.

Milwaukee Board of Fire and Police Commissioners. *Commemorative Booklet 1885–1985: A Matter of Experiment*, 1985.

Milwaukee Daily Journal. Nineteenth Century U.S. Newspapers. Thomsen Gale Infotrac. Brigham Young University Family History Archive. www.lib.byu.edu (accessed on July 14, 2007).

Milwaukee Daily Sentinel. Nineteenth Century U.S. Newspapers. Thomsen Gale Infotrac. Brigham Young University Family History Archive. www.lib.byu.edu (accessed on July 14, 2007).

Milwaukee Police Association. *Milwaukee Badge: Special Memorial Edition, 1884–1986*. Milwaukee: 1986.

National Police Journal. VIII, no. 2 (June 1921).

Retired Police Association of Milwaukee. *Wisconsin Law Enforcement Annual*. Various years.

Still, Bayrd. *Milwaukee: The History of a City*. Madison: State Historical Society of Wisconsin, 1965.